W9-CNN-300

WINNING CASINO BLACKJACK FOR THE NON-COUNTER

A STEP-BY-STEP MANUAL FOR BLACKJACK PLAYERS

"His candor ... is refreshing in its honesty ... For the casual player who is not inclined to devote the time necessary for mastering a count strategy, this is the best book I've seen of its type."

ARNOLD SNYDER
First-round member of the Blackjack Hall of Fame
Author of *Blackbelt in Blackjack*, *Big Book of Blackjack*

"I've seen all the best, and Avery Cardoza ranks as one of the greatest blackjack players in the world. This book will make any beginning player a winner."

EDWIN SILBERSTANG
Gambling legend and author of over 20 gaming books
including *Winning Blackjack for Serious Players*

To My Father

WINNING CASINO BLACKJACK FOR THE NON-COUNTER

A STEP-BY-STEP MANUAL FOR BLACKJACK PLAYERS

AVERY CARDOZA

CARDOZA PUBLISHING

Cardoza Publishing is the foremost gaming and gambling publisher in the world with a library of more than 200 up-to-date and easy-to-read books and strategies. These authoritative works are written by the top experts in their fields and with more than 10,000,000 books in print, represent the best-selling and most popular gaming books anywhere.

2010 NEW EDITION!

Copyright©1981, 1986, 1992, 1999, 2002, 2005, 2010 by Avery Cardoza

Library of Congress Catalog Number: 2010921133
ISBN 10:   1-58042-243-8
ISBN 13: 978-1-58042-243-7

Visit our website or write for a full list of Cardoza Publishing books and advanced strategies.

CARDOZA PUBLISHING

P.O. Box 98115, Las Vegas, NV 89193
Toll-Free Phone (800)577-WINS
email: cardozabooks@aol.com
www.cardozabooks.com

ABOUT THE AUTHOR

Avery Cardoza is the foremost gambling authority in the world and best-selling author of twenty-one gambling books and advanced strategies, including *How to Win at Gambling, Secrets of Winning Slots,* and the classic, *Winning Casino Blackjack for the Non-Counter.* Millions of players have learned how to play and win money at gambling following his no-nonsense practical advice.

Cardoza began his gambling career underage in Las Vegas as a professional blackjack player beating the casinos at their own game and was soon barred from one casino after another. In 1981, when even the biggest casinos refused him play, Cardoza founded Cardoza Publishing, the foremost and largest gaming publisher in the world. Cardoza Publishing, which is the home of many of the giants in the world of gambling, has published more than 200 gaming titles and sold more than ten million books.

Though originally from Brooklyn, New York, where he is occasionally found, Cardoza has used his winnings to pursue a lifestyle of extensive traveling in exotic locales around the world.

Visit www.cardozabooks.com for a full list of Cardoza Publishing books.

CONTENTS

TABLE OF CONTENTS

TABLES

INTRODUCTION TO
THE REVISED EDITION

This new edition has greatly increased in size to reflect the latest information on winning money at blackjack and to show you how to beat blackjack games anywhere in the world! There are more questions and answers to help you understand the big picture and the nuances of beating the game of 21, more information on getting that extra edge, and more frank discussion on finding the right games to beat including ones that should be avoided.

I've kept the same approach that has made this book a modern classic for winning at blackjack and best-seller for almost thirty years. After clearly explaining the rules, variations and how the game is played I get right to the heart of the matter—how to win money at blackjack. Winning strategies are presented three ways for you to learn. First, I show the underlying principles of the strategies and explain concepts such as stiff cards, pat cards and the ten factor.

Then, I present the strategies in mini-chart form and the thinking behind each move so that you learn why each play is made. I call this thinking process, "conceptual blackjack." Finally, to make sure the winning strategies are crystal clear, I present the Cardoza Master Charts to cover the correct plays for all blackjack games wherever you may find them!

This book is not just about showing you how to be a winner, but also, how to understand the game and be a thinking player.

I could have called this book the *Thinking Person's Guide to Blackjack*. If you understand *why* you should make the proper plays, then you have a great chance to make the proper plays when you need to. And that will count for money in your pocket in the long run.

This book emphasizes winning, and that's what we're here to do now—win at blackjack!

INTRODUCTION

Blackjack can be beaten! Once you've finished reading this book and learned the skills presented, you'll find that there will be one major difference between you and 95% of the other players—you'll be a winner at blackjack!

I'll teach you how to win without the blind memorization and boring tedium usually associated with learning blackjack. The computer-tested basic strategies are carefully explained so that every play you make is easily learned. In addition, all the winning strategies are presented in easy-to-read charts.

You'll learn how to beat the single-deck game without counting cards and how best to adjust your play for multiple-deck games whether you're a player in Las Vegas, Northern Nevada, Atlantic City, the Mississippi riverboats and Indian reservations, or you're heading for play in Europe, Asia, the Bahamas, the Caribbean, or anywhere else blackjack is found.

You'll receive a wealth of information from this book. I cover the fundamentals of casino blackjack—the rules of the game, the player's options, the variations offered in casinos around the world, how to bet, casino jargon, how to play and everything else you'll need to know about playing winning casino blackjack.

Not only will I teach you the skills of winning, but just as important, I'll teach you how to walk away a winner. Money management is carefully explained to insure your success as a blackjack player. I also discuss emotional control, how to minimize losses when losing, and how to let your winnings ride, so that when you lose, you lose small, and when you win, you win big—the overall result being that you walk away a winner!

For the first time, the winning concepts that have been successfully taught at the Cardoza School of Blackjack are now presented here so that you can win without counting cards.

So read this book carefully, and you'll be among those players that the casinos fear, and for good reason—you will be a consistent winner at blackjack!

BEGINNER'S GUIDE TO CASINO BLACKJACK

OBJECT OF THE GAME

Your object in casino blackjack is to beat the dealer. This can be achieved in two ways:

- When you have a higher total than the dealer without exceeding 21.
- When the dealer's total exceeds 21 (assuming the player has not exceeded 21 first).

In casino blackjack, if the player and the dealer both hold the same total of 21 or less, the hand is a **push**, nobody wins.

BUSTING OR BREAKING— AUTOMATIC LOSERS

If the drawing of additional cards to the initial two cards dealt causes the point total to exceed 21, then that hand is said to be **busted**, an automatic loss. Busted hands should be turned up immediately. Once you have busted, your hand is lost, even if the dealer busts as well afterwards. If the dealer busts, all remaining players automatically win their bets.

BLACKJACK—AUTOMATIC WINNER

If the original two-card hand contains an ace with any 10 or face card (J, Q, K), the hand is called a **blackjack**, or **natural**, and is an automatic winner for the player. Blackjacks used to be universally paid off at 3 to 2, though some casinos today pay only 6 to 5, a change that is very detrimental to your winning chances. (In fact, I recommend that you avoid any game that pays 6 to 5 on blackjacks because it costs you 1.39% compared to the standard 3 to 2 payoff.)

If the dealer gets a blackjack, all players lose their bets. The dealer wins only the player's bet, not the 3 to 2 or 6 to 5 the player receives for his blackjack. If both the dealer and the player are dealt a blackjack, the hand is a push.

Blackjacks should be turned up immediately. They will be paid off and the cards removed by the dealer before the other players get to act on their hands.

PAYOFFS

All bets are paid off at even money (for example, a $5 bet wins $5), except in cases where you are dealt a blackjack which is paid at either 3 to 2 ($5 bet wins $7.50) or at 6 to 5 ($5 bet wins $6)—or when you exercise an option that allows you to double your bet. In these instances (doubling and splitting), the payoff is equal to the new doubled bet. If a bet is doubled from $5 to $10, a win would pay off $10.

CARD VALUES

Blackjack is played with a standard deck of cards, or up to eight decks shuffled together. Each card in the deck is counted at face value; 2 equals 2 points, 3 equals 3 points, and a 10 equals 10 points. The face cards, jack, queen and king, are counted as 10 points. The ace can be counted as 1 point or 11 points at the player's discretion. When the ace is counted as 11 points, that hand is called **soft**, as in the hand A7, which is a *soft 18*. All other totals, including hands where the ace counts as 1 point, are called **hard**, as in the hands 107 and 106A, which are both *hard* 17s.

DEALER'S RULES

The dealer must play by prescribed guidelines. He must draw to any hand 16 or below and stand on any total 17-21. The dealer must count his ace as 11 points if that gives him a hand totaling 17 through 21, otherwise he must count the ace as 1 point.

In some casinos the rules dictate that the dealer must draw on soft 17. In these casinos, the dealer's ace will count as 1 point when combined with cards totalling 6 points, for example, the dealer will have to draw with the hand of A23 (a soft 16) until he forms a hand of at least hard 17.

The dealer has no playing options and cannot deviate from the above-stated rules.

PLAYER'S OPTIONS

Unlike the dealer, you can vary your strategy. After receiving your first two cards, you have the following options:

1. Drawing (Hitting)

If you are not satisfied with your two-card total, you can draw additional cards. To draw a card, you scrape the felt surface with your cards, scraping toward your body. In a game where both the player's cards are dealt face up, you are not supposed to touch the cards and instead you scratch the felt with your index finger or point toward the cards if you desire an additional card or cards.

2. Standing

When you are satisfied with your hand and do not wish to draw additional cards, you signal this by sliding your cards face down under your bet. When the cards are dealt face up, you indicate your decision to stand pat by waving your hand palm down over your cards.

3. Doubling Down

This option allows you to double your original bet, in which case you *must* draw one additional card to your hand and cannot draw any more cards thereafter. To double down, you turn your cards face up and place them in front of your bet. Then you take an amount equal to your original bet and places those chips next to that bet, so that there are now two equivalent bets side by side. In games where the cards are dealt face up, you simply place the additional bet next to your original one to indicate the double down.

The dealer will then deal one card face down, usually slipping that card under your bet. You may look at that card if you desire. In games where both player cards are dealt face up, this card is usually dealt face up.

4. Splitting Pairs

If you're dealt two cards of equivalent rank, such as 33, 77, 88 (any combination of 10, J, Q, K is considered a pair), you can split these cards so that two separate hands are formed. To split a pair, you turn your pair face up, separate them, putting each card in its own place in front of your bet. You then place a bet equal to the original wager behind the second hand. Each hand is played separately, using finger and hand signals to indicate hitting and standing.

In games where both your cards are dealt face up, the split is indicated by placing the additional bet next to the original one. You use hand signals as above to indicate hitting or standing.

If the first card dealt to either split hand has a value identical to the original split cards, that card may be split again (**resplit**) into a third hand, with the exception of aces. When you split aces, you receive only one card on each ace and may not draw again, no matter what card is drawn. Note that a 10 drawn to a split ace is not a blackjack, but simply a 21. Only an original holding of an ace and a 10 is considered a blackjack.

5. Doubling Down After Splitting

You can double down on one or both of the hands resulting from a split according to the normal doubling rules of the casino. This option is offered in all Atlantic City casinos and in certain Nevada casinos. It is also found in Australia, Great Britain, various European and Asian casinos, and southern Africa.

For example, if a pair of 8s are split, and a 3 is drawn to the first 8 for an 11, you may elect to double down on that 11. You do so by placing an amount equal to the original bet next to the 11. You'll receive only one additional card for that hand. The other 8 is played separately and can be doubled as well should an advantageous card such as a 2 or 3 be drawn.

Since options allowed are often in flux, sometimes changing from one month to the next, always ask the rules that are in play, even if you have previously played in the casino, so that you can take advantage of any options that may benefit you.

6. Surrender (Late Surrender)

You may "surrender" your original two-card hand and forfeit one half of your bet after it has been determined that the dealer does not have a blackjack. This option is frequently allowed in Asia and the Caribbean, while in the United States, surrender is offered in only a few casinos.

To surrender, you turn both your cards face up, put them above your bet, and say "surrender." In a game where both your cards are dealt face up, you announce your intention verbally to the dealer.

The dealer will collect the cards and take one half of the bet.

7. Early Surrender

This is a player option that allows you to give up your hand and lose half your bet *before* the dealer checks for a blackjack. This very favorable option was originally introduced in Atlantic City but is no longer offered because of subsequent changes in Atlantic City rules.

8. Insurance

If the dealer shows an ace as his upcard, he will ask the players if they want insurance. If you exercise this option, you are betting that the dealer has a 10-value card (10, J, Q, or K) as his hole card—a blackjack. To take insurance, you place up to one-half the amount of your bet in the area marked "insurance." If the dealer does indeed have a blackjack, you get paid 2 to 1 on the insurance bet, while losing the original bet. In effect, the transaction is a standoff, and no money is lost. If the dealer does not have a blackjack, the insurance bet is lost and play continues.

If you hold a blackjack and take insurance on the dealer's ace, the payoff will be even-money whether the dealer has a blackjack or not. Suppose you have a $10 bet and take insurance for $5 on your blackjack. If the dealer has a blackjack, you win 2 to 1 on your $5 insurance bet and tie with your own blackjack. If the dealer doesn't have a blackjack, you lose the $5 insurance bet but get paid 3 to 2 on your blackjack. Either way you win $10. To make it easy, you can just say "Even Money," and the dealer will pay you off at even money and collect the cards.

INSURANCE STRATEGY

Though you might often hear otherwise from "experienced" players, insurance is a bad bet. Making an insurance wager is betting that the dealer has a 10 under his ace. Since the insurance payoff is 2 to 1, the wager will only be a profitable option for you when the ratio of tens to other cards is either equal to or less than 2 to 1.

Let's break down a pack of 52 cards to see how this works. A full deck has 36 non-tens and 16 tens, a ratio greater than 2 to 1. If the first deal off the top of the deck gives us a hand of 97, and the dealer shows an ace, then we know three cards, all non-tens. Now the ratio of non-tens to tens is 33 to 16, still greater than 2 to 1, and still a poor bet. If, instead, you were dealt two tens (for a 20), then the ratio is 35 to 14, an even worse bet.

In a multiple-deck game, taking insurance is also a poor bet, more costly even than in a single-deck game, and shouldn't be made.

INSURING A BLACKJACK

Taking insurance when you have a blackjack is also a bad bet, despite the well intentioned advice of dealers and other players to always insure a blackjack. Let's go back to the basic math. When you have a blackjack, you know three cards, your 10 and ace, and the dealer's ace. The already poor starting ratio of 36 tens to 16 non-tens gets worse, becoming 34 to 15 in a single-deck game.

Taking insurance when you have a blackjack gives the house an 8% advantage, a poor proposition for you. That's worse than any roulette bet you can make; in fact, it is significantly worse than most of the bets you'll find at table games in the casinos.

THE PLAY OF THE GAME

The dealer begins by shuffling the cards and offering the cut to one of the players. If refused, it is offered to another player. The dealer then completes the cut, and removes the top card, called the **burn card**. In single- and double-deck games, the burn card is either put under the deck face up, where all subsequent cards will be placed, or is put face down into a plastic case (procedures vary from casino to casino) to be followed similarly by future discards.

In games dealt out of a shoe, the burn card will be placed most of the way into the shoe and discards will be put in the plastic case situated to the right of the dealer.

Players must make their bets before the cards are dealt

The dealer deals clockwise from his left to his right, one card at a time, until each player and the dealer have received two cards. The players cards are usually dealt face down in a single or double-deck game, though it makes no difference if they are dealt face up as they usually are in a game dealt out of a shoe, for the dealer is bound by strict rules from which he cannot deviate. The dealer deals only one of his two cards face up. This card is called an **upcard**. The face down card is known as the **hole card** or the **downcard**.

If the dealer's upcard is an ace, he will ask the players if they want insurance. Players that opt to take insurance, place a bet of up to one-half their wager in the area marked "insurance," which is located on the layout between their bet and the dealer.

If the dealer has a blackjack, all players that did not take insurance lose their bets. Players that took insurance break even on the play. If the dealer doesn't have a blackjack, he collects the lost insurance bets and play continues.

The procedures vary when the dealer shows a 10-value card. In many Nevada casinos the dealer must check his hole card for an ace. If he has a blackjack, it is an automatic winner for the house. All player bets are lost. (Players can't insure against a 10-value card.) Players that hold blackjack push on the play. If the dealer doesn't have a blackjack, he will face the first player and await that player's decision. (In Atlantic City, the Bahamas and most European games, the dealer will only check the hole card after all the players have acted.)

Play begins with the bettor on the dealer's immediate left, in the position known as **first base**. If no player is seated there, then the player sitting in the first available seat to the left of first base will begin play.

The first player to act has the option to stand, hit, double down, split (if he has two cards of equal value) or surrender (if allowed). A player may draw cards until he is satisfied with his total or busts, or he may exercise one of the other options just mentioned.

Play moves to the next player. If a player busts (goes over 21) or receives a blackjack, he must turn over his cards immediately. If a bust, the dealer will collect the lost bet. If a blackjack, the dealer will pay 3 to 2 (or 6 to 5, depending upon whether the casino has instituted this unpopular payoff)) on the won bet.

After the last player has acted upon his cards, the dealer will turn his hole card over so that all players can view both of his cards. He must play his hand according to the strict guidelines regulating his play; drawing to 17 or better, then standing. (In some casinos the dealer must draw to a soft 17.) If the dealer busts, that is, his total goes over 21, all players still in the game for that round of play win automatically.

After playing his hand, the dealer will turn over each player's cards in turn, going counterclockwise from his right to his left, the opposite direction from how he dealt, paying the winners, and collecting from the losers. Once a bettor has played his hand, he shouldn't touch his cards again. He should let the dealer expose his hand which he will do once the dealer has played out his own hand.

The above procedure described a single- or double-deck game, where players cards were dealt face down. In a multiple-deck game, play would proceed as just described except that players cards would be face up the whole time.

When the round has been completed, all players must place a new bet before the next deal.

CASINO PERSONNEL

The casino employee responsible for the running of the blackjack game is called the **dealer**. The dealer's duties are to deal the cards to the players, and play out his own hand according to the rules of the game. He converts money into chips for players entering the game or buying in for more chips during the course of play, makes the correct payoffs for winning hands, and collects bets from the losers.

The dealer's supervisor—technically called the **floorman**, but more commonly referred to as the **pit boss**—is responsible for the supervision of between four to six tables. He makes sure the games are run smoothly and he settles any disputes that may arise with a player. More importantly, his job is to oversee the exchange of money and to correct any errors that may occur.

ENTERING A GAME

To enter a blackjack game, sit down at any unoccupied seat at the blackjack table, and place the money you wish to gamble with near the betting box in front of you. You don't want to place your chips on the betting box itself because that would be considered a bet! Unless betting the entire amount you've placed on the table is your intention, you want to be careful that the dealer knows you are only exchanging your cash for chips. You can make extra sure of this by verbally informing the dealer that you would like chips, though that request will be perfectly understood when your cash is placed on the felt, but not in a betting area.

Chips may be purchased in various denominations. Let the dealer know which chips or combination of chips you'd like.

The dealer will take your money and call out the amount he is changing so that the pit boss is aware that a transaction is taking place and can supervise that exchange.

CONVERTING TRAVELER'S CHECKS AND MONEY ORDERS TO CASH

The dealers will accept only cash or chips, so if you bring traveler's checks, money orders or the like, you must go to the area of the casino marked **Casino Cashier** to get these converted to cash. Be sure to bring proper identification to insure a smooth transaction.

CASINO CHIPS

Standard denominations of casino chips are $1, $5, $25, $100 and for the high rollers, $500, $1,000 and even higher denomination chips can be obtained. Though some casinos use their own color code, the usual color scheme of chips are as shown in the following chart:

TYPICAL CHIP COLORS

Chip Value	Color	Nickname
$1	White, Blue*	Silver
$5	Red	Nickel, Redbird
$25	Green	Quarter
$100	Black	Dollar
$500	Purple	Barney
$1,000	Orange	Pumpkin

*$1 chips universally used to be silver tokens, and they can still occasionally be found, though the standard today is for the $1 chips to be white or blue in color and composed of clay or plastic.

BETTING

Casinos prefer that the players use chips for betting purposes, for the handling of money at the tables is cumbersome and slows the game. While cash can be used for wagers, all payoffs will be in chips.

To bet, place your chips (or cash) in the betting box directly in front of you. All bets must be placed before the cards are dealt.

HOUSE LIMITS

Placards located at either corner of the table indicate the minimum and maximum bets allowed at a particular table. Within the same casino you may find minimums ranging from $1, $2 and $5, to $25 or even $100 per hand. Some casinos, trying to attract the low-rolling crowd might even, on occasion, offer 25¢ blackjack games. On the other end of the spectrum, private tables are sometimes set up for high rollers who'll bet minimums of $5,000 or higher per bet.

At the $5 or less minimum tables, the house maximum generally will not exceed $500 to $1,000 while the $25 and $100 tables may allow the players to bet as high as $3,000 a hand or higher. In ultra-high stakes games, the high roller will usually arrange in advance a limit with the casino.

CONVERTING CHIPS INTO CASH

Even though dealers will take your cash and convert it into chips, they do not perform the exchange the other way around. To convert chips back into cash, you'll have to go to the cashier's cage where that exchange will be done for you.

TIPPING

Tipping, or **toking**, as it is called in casino parlance, should be viewed as a gratuitous gesture to a dealer you feel has given you good service. Toking is totally at your discretion, and in no way should be considered an obligation. It is not your duty to support casino employees, though it is customary for winning players to show appreciation after a good session.

If you're inclined to recognize good service, toke only when you're winning, and only to dealers who are friendly and helpful to you. Do not toke dealers that you don't like or ones that try to make you feel guilty about not tipping. Dealers that make playing an unpleasant experience for you deserve nothing.

The best way to tip a dealer is to place a bet for the dealer in front of your own bet, so that his chances of winning that toke are tied up with your hand. If the hand is won, you both win together; if the hand is lost, you lose together. By being partners on the hand, you establish camaraderie with the dealer. Naturally, he or she will be rooting for you to win. This is the best way to tip, for when you win, the dealer wins double—the tip amount you bet plus the winnings from that bet.

CHEATING

It is my belief that cheating is not a problem in the major American gambling centers, though I would not totally eliminate the possibility. If you ever feel uncomfortable about the honesty of a game, stop playing. Though you probably are being dealt an honest game, the anxiety of being uncomfortable is not worth the action. If you're worried about being cheated, that anxiety will hang over you and will negatively affect your game. Additionally, you certainly won't be enjoying your time at the table.

Do not confuse bad luck with being cheated, or a dealer's mistake as chicanery. Dealers have a difficult job and work hard. They are bound to make honest mistakes. If you find yourself shorted on a payoff, bring it immediately to the dealer's attention and the mistake will be corrected.

FREE DRINKS AND CIGARETTES

Casinos offer their customers unlimited free drinking while playing at the table. In addition to alcoholic beverages, you can order milk, soft drinks, juices or any other beverages. This is ordered through and served by a cocktail waitress.

Cigarettes and cigars are also complimentary and can be ordered through the cocktail waitress.

THE DECKS OF CARDS

Nevada casinos use one, two, four, six and sometimes as many as eight decks of cards in their blackjack games. Often, within the same casino, single and multiple-deck games will be offered.

Typically though, outside of Nevada, multiple-deck blackjack dealt out of a shoe is the standard of play in the world whether played in Atlantic City, Europe, Asia, South America, the Bahamas, the Caribbean, on casino boats, or anywhere else blackjack may be found. Atlantic City casinos, however, occasionally offer single-deck blackjack as well. When one or two decks are used, the dealer holds the cards in his hand. When more than two decks are used, the cards are dealt from a rectangular plastic or wooden device known as a **shoe**. The shoe is designed to hold multiple decks, and allows the cards to be easily removed one at a time by the dealer.

Each deck used in blackjack is a standard pack of 52 cards, consisting of four cards of each value, ace through king. Suits have no relevance in blackjack. Only the numerical value of the cards count. Thus, for example, if four decks are used, there will be 16 cards of each value in play, and similarly, if six decks are in play, there will be 24 cards (six decks x four for each rank) of each value.

STANDEES

In some areas around the world, most notably Europe and Asia, **standees**, players not occupying a seat and betting spot at the table, are allowed to place bets in the boxes of players already seated. However, standees must accept the seated player's decision and are not allowed to advise or criticize the play made.

NO-HOLE-CARD RULE

The predominant style of play in casinos outside the United States is for the dealer to take his second card after all the players have acted upon their hands. In some cases, the dealer may deal himself the card as in the U.S. casinos, but will not check a 10 or an ace for blackjack until after the bettors have finished playing their hands.

The disadvantage to the player is that on hands doubled or split, the additional moneys bet will be lost if indeed the dealer has a blackjack. As you'll see, we'll adjust our strategies accordingly when playing in no-hole-card games, being less aggressive in doubling and splitting situations so we can minimize the negative effect of this rule. In some U.S. casinos, blackjack is played in this style. The difference in these games though, is that when the dealer has a blackjack, the player's additional bets on doubles and splits are returned. Only the original bet will be lost. Thus, this style is not a disadvantage to players.

It is only when our additional bets are not returned, as in the regular no-hole-card games, that we adjust our strategies.

RULES AND VARIATIONS OF THE CASINO CENTERS

Blackjack can be found all over the world, and though basically the same wherever played, the rules and variations vary from country to country, from casino to casino within a country, and sometimes, they even differ within a casino itself.

NEVADA RULES

The Las Vegas Strip rules are advantageous to the player and gives one a slight edge on the single-deck game if our strategies are followed. The rule exceptions noted in Downtown Las Vegas and in Northern Nevada games are slightly disadvantageous to the player, but these can easily be overcome by using the winning techniques presented later.

LAS VEGAS STRIP RULES

- Dealer must draw on all totals of 16 or less, and stand on all totals of 17-21.
- Player may take insurance on a dealer's ace.
- Insurance payoffs are 2 to 1.

- Player receives a 3 to 2 payoff on his blackjack.*
- Player may double down on any initial two card combination.
- Identical pairs may be split, resplit, and drawn to as desired with the exception of split aces, on which the player is allowed only one hit on each ace.
- One, two, four and bigger deck games are standard.

DOWNTOWN LAS VEGAS RULES

Rules are the same as the Las Vegas Strip rules with one exception:

- Dealer must draw to soft 17.

NORTHERN NEVADA RULES

Same as Las Vegas Strip rules with two exceptions:

- Dealer must draw to soft 17.
- Doubling is restricted to two-card totals of 10 and 11 only.

ATLANTIC CITY RULES

The New Jersey Casino Control Commission regulates the rules and variations of the casinos under its jurisdiction. Atlantic City casinos must abide by the following guidelines:

- Dealer must draw to all totals 16 or less and stand on all totals of 17-21. Many casinos now offer games where dealer has to draw on soft 17.

---

* Note that 6 to 5 payoffs for blackjacks are sometimes offered instead. It is a terrible rule which costs you 1.39% compared to the 3 to 2 payoff. I advise you to avoid these games.

- Player may take insurance on a dealer's ace. Insurance payoffs are 2 to 1.
- Player receives a 3 to 2 payoff on his blackjack.*
- Player may double on any initial two-card combination.
- Identical pairs may be resplit.
- Doubling after splitting allowed.
- Four, six and eight decks are standard. One-deck games are occasionally offered.*

EUROPEAN RULES

Blackjack is offered in numerous countries around Europe with the rules and variations changing slightly from place to place. However, the following conditions apply in a good many of these places.

- Dealer must draw to all totals 16 or less, and stand on all totals of 17-21.
- Player may take insurance on a dealer's ace.
- Insurance payoffs are 2 to 1.
- Player receives a 3 to 2 payoff on his blackjack.
- Doubling down on 9-11 only
- Standees permitted
- No-hole-card rule
- 4-6 decks standard
- If player draws a 2 on an A8 double down hand, total counts as 11, not 21

---

* Note that 6 to 5 payoffs for blackjacks are offered on their single-deck games. It is a terrible rule which costs you 1.39% compared to the 3 to 2 payoff. I advise you to avoid these games.

RULES AROUND THE WORLD
Bahamas • Caribbean • Europe • Southern Africa • Asia
South America • Other Locations

The general blackjack variations we presented for the European Rules, above, are the most prevalent style of rules you'll find in casinos around the world. Sometimes you may find double after split permitted as in Great Britain, southern Africa, many European casinos and other places. In Asian and Caribbean casinos, surrender is often allowed.

It's always a good idea to learn the particular rules of a game before playing so you know what you're up against and how best to play your hands.

BLACKJACK IS BLACKJACK

Note that single-deck blackjack is hard to find outside the Nevada casinos. Multiple-deck blackjack is the predominant style of play in casinos around the world and the type of game you'll most likely face when you take on the casinos at blackjack.

However, no matter where you play, the game of blackjack is basically the same give or take some minor options, and we'll show you how to win against any variation.

GENERAL STRATEGIC CONCEPTS

THE DEALER'S ONLY ADVANTAGE

Before we examine the correct strategies of play, it would be instructive to look at a losing strategy. In this strategy, the player will mimic the dealer; he'll draw on all totals 16 or less, and stand on all totals 17-21.*

The player doing this figures that since this strategy wins for the dealer, it must be effective for the player as well. After all, the dealer and the player will get the same number of good hands and the same number of poor hands. And if we draw just as the dealer draws, we must come out even, mustn't we?

No. As a matter of fact, the player will be playing at about a 5½% disadvantage to the house. The "Mimic the Dealer" strategy overlooks one important thing: The player *must* act upon his hand first.

The dealer's only advantage lies in the fact that once the player has busted, the player's bet is automatically lost, regardless of the outcome of the dealer's hand. While both the dealer and the player will bust equally following these drawing-to-17 guidelines (about 28% of the time), the double bust, where both the dealer and the player bust on the same round, will occur approximately 8% of the time (28% of 28% of the time

---

* Roger Baldwin, Wilbert Cantey, Herbert Maisel, and James McDermott, in their classic book, *Playing Blackjack to Win*, originally discussed the "Mimic the Dealer" concept back in 1957.

or 28 x 28). And since the player acted first, this 8% of the time (the double bust) will be the house advantage.

When we adjust for the 3 to 2 bonus the player receives on blackjacks, a bonus the house does not enjoy, we find the house enjoying a 5½% edge over the player that follows the "Mimic the Dealer" Strategy.

OVERCOMING THE DISADVANTAGE OF ACTING FIRST

In the "Mimic the Dealer" strategy we played our hands as if our goal was to get as close to 21 as reasonably possible by using 17 as a cutoff point for drawing. But this losing strategy misstates the goal of the player. In blackjack, the object is to beat the dealer. Our chances of winning are not determined by how close our total approaches 21 as the other strategy assumed, but on how good our total is compared to the dealer's total.

We can overcome the disadvantage of having to act first by making judicious use of the options available to us as a player. Not only should we double down, split pairs, hit, stand and surrender (if allowed), but we can use our knowledge of the dealer's exposed upcard to fully capitalize on these options. Needless to say, adjusting our strategy according to this knowledge of the dealer's upcard will vastly improve on the "Get as Close to 21—Mimic the Dealer" strategy, and completely eliminate the house edge.

TO BEAT THE DEALER

There are two factors that affect our chances of winning; the strength of our total and the strength of the dealer's total. To beat the dealer, we must know how strong our total is compared to the dealer's total so that we know if drawing additional cards or exercising a player option is a viable consideration. In addition, we must be aware of the factors that influence the final outcome of these totals so that we can determine the optimal strategy.

In determining the best way to play our hand, we must know how good our total is as it stands.

- Do we have the expectancy of winning by standing?
- If so, can we increase this expectancy by drawing additional cards or by exercising a doubling or splitting option when applicable?
- If we do not have the expectancy of winning by standing, will the drawing of additional cards or the employment of the doubling or splitting option increase our chance of winning?

Since our object is to beat the dealer, to answer the question, "How strong is our total?" we need to ask ourselves if the dealer's expectancy, judged by the information we get from his exposed card, is greater than our total.

Being able to see the dealer's upcard gives us a great deal of information about the strength of the hands that the dealer is likely to make, and we can use that information to our advantage.

THE TEN FACTOR

The most striking feature of blackjack is the dominant role that the 10-value cards (10, J, Q, K) play, what we call the **ten factor**. Each 10 and face card is counted as 10 points in blackjack. It is important to consider that you are four times more likely to draw a 10 than any other individual card since aces through nines consist of only 4 cards each as opposed to 16 tens. Collectively, the tens constitute just under 1/3 of the deck (16 out of 52 cards).

Because the tens are such a dominant factor in a deck of cards, it's correct to think of the dealer's hand as gravitating toward a total 10 points greater than his exposed upcard. When I speak of a hand as *gravitating* toward a total, I am referring to the tendency of that hand to increase in value by 10 points as a result of the ten factor. Thus, for example, starting out with an upcard of 9, the dealer will make a hand of 19 about 36% of the time and 19 or better 52% of the time.

UNDERSTANDING THE DEALER'S UPCARD

Being able to see the dealer's upcard is of great value to us for there are two factors—the rules governing the dealer's play of his hand, and the number of tens in a deck of cards (ten factor)—that tell us a great deal about the potential strength of the dealer's hands, and the frequency with which those hands will bust.

THE DEALER'S RULES AND THE TEN FACTOR

Our strategy is based on the fact that the dealer must play by prescribed guidelines from which he cannot deviate. He must draw to all totals 16 or below, and stand on all totals 17-21 (except in casinos that require the dealer to draw to soft 17). All hard totals that exceed hard 21 are automatic dealer losses.

The combination of the ten factor with the dealer's rigid drawing and standing rules creates a natural separation of the dealer's upcard into two distinct groupings: 2s through 6s, the dealer **stiff cards**, and 7s through aces, the dealer **pat cards**.

We'll base our strategies accordingly.

2s THROUGH 6s— DEALER STIFF CARDS

Whenever the dealer shows a 2, 3, 4, 5 or 6 as an upcard, we know that he must draw at least one additional card regardless of the value of his hole card (unless the dealer has an ace under his 6 and is playing Las Vegas Strip, Atlantic city or European style rules which require the dealer to stand on soft 17). The high concentration of tens in the deck often lead to the dealer exposing a 10 as his hole card, giving him a stiff total of 12-16.

Since the dealer must draw to all hard totals 16 or below, the drawing of a 10 (and in some instances, smaller valued cards) will bust any of these stiff totals. For example, if the dealer shows a 6 and reveals a 10 in the hole, any card higher than a 5 will bust his hand.

Thus, the high concentration of 10-value cards in the deck tells us that the dealer has a good chance of busting when his upcard is a 2, 3, 4, 5 or 6.

UNDERSTANDING THE DEALER'S STIFF CARDS				
Dealer Stiff Cards—Advantageous for Player				
2 3		4	5	6
Less Advantageous		More Advantageous		

Dealer's Upcard of 2 and 3

Though it is favorable for the player when the dealer shows a 2 or 3 as an upcard, we will need to be cautious against these stiff cards, for the dealer will bust less often with these than when he shows the 4, 5 or 6.

Dealer's Upcard of 4, 5 and 6

The dealer is showing the upcards you always want him to hold. The dealer will bust about 42% of the time with these upcards (about 5% more than the 2 or 3, and about 18% more than with the pat cards). We will take advantage of these weak dealer upcards by aggressive splitting and doubling.

7s THROUGH ACES— DEALER PAT CARDS

Whenever the dealer shows a 7, 8, 9, 10 or ace as an upcard, we know, because of the large number of tens, that he has a high likelihood of making pat totals 17-21, and conversely, a smaller chance of busting than when he shows a stiff card. This high concentration of tens often lead to the dealer exposing a 10 for an automatic pat hand (17-21). Even when he doesn't have a 10 in the hole, combinations such as 89, A7, 99, and so forth, give the dealer an automatic pat hand as well.

UNDERSTANDING THE DEALER'S PAT CARDS	
Dealer Pat Cards—Disadvantageous for Player	
7 8 9	10 Ace
Moderately Disadvantageous	Very Disadvantageous

Dealer's Upcard of 7 and 8

While the dealer will not bust often with these upcards, they also indicate to us that the dealer's hands gravitate toward the weaker totals of 17 and 18. It is interesting to note that of all the dealer upcards, including the stiff cards, the 7 will form the weakest totals.

Dealer's Upcard of 9, 10 and Ace

The 9 and 10 gravitate toward totals of 19 and 20 respectively—tough hands to beat. The ace is also a powerful dealer upcard, for in addition to forming strong hands, the dealer will bust less with an ace than with any other upcard.

Against these powerful upcards, we will be very cautious in our doubling and splitting strategies.

UNDERSTANDING THE PLAYER'S HAND–HARD TOTALS

The player's totals can be divided into three distinct groupings: 11 or less, 17-21 and 12-16.

We will look at each in turn to see how they affect our strategy, but first, let's examine the player's pat hand totals to get a better feel for the reasoning behind the strategy plays we'll make.

UNDERSTANDING THE PLAYER'S PAT HAND TOTALS				
17	18	19	20	21
poor	fair	good	excellent	excellent

When you realize that overall, the dealer will average better than an 18 for each hand played, you see why the final total of 18 is classified in our scale as no better than a fair total, and that 17 is quite clearly a poor one. The total of 19 is a good hand, while 20 and 21, as all blackjack player's know, are excellent totals that we'd love to have hand after hand.

Player's Hand of 11 or Less (Hard Totals)

We should always draw to any hard total 11 or less (unless a doubling or splitting option is more profitable). By hitting these hands we have no risk of busting no matter what we draw, and the drawing of a card can strengthen our total.

There is no question about the correct decision; drawing is always a big gain.

Player's Hand of 17-21 (Hard Totals)

We should always stand on these hard totals (17-21), for the risk of busting is too high to make drawing worthwhile. It should be obvious that the chances of improving these strong hands are minimal, and the risks of busting very probable. In addition, totals of 19, 20, and 21 are already powerful hands, while 18, to a lesser extent, is a good playable total.

On the other hand, while hard 17 is a poor player total, the risk of busting by drawing is way too costly to make this a viable option.

Stand on hard totals of 17-21 against any dealer's upcard.

Player's Hand of 12-16 (Hard Totals)

With these hands the bulk of our decision making will be exercised, for on these hard totals there are no automatic decisions as on the other player totals.

Our hand is not an obvious draw (such as the 11 or less grouping) for the risk of drawing a 10 or other high card and busting is substantial. Our hand is not an obvious stand decision either (such as the 17-21 grouping), for the only times we will win with these weak totals of 12-16 are the times that the dealer busts.

We discuss this grouping in the following chapter, the *Optimal Basic Strategies*, where we show you the correct way to play every hand dealt in blackjack, and later, in *The Winning Edge* chapter, show you how to use this information to be a winner at blackjack.

GENERAL STRATEGIC CONCEPTS

For the Cardoza Non-Counter winning strategies to be effective (or any other strategy for that matter) and for you to be a winner at blackjack, you must first know the correct way to play all your hands, so read the following chapters carefully.

Let's get to it!

THE OPTIMAL BASIC STRATEGIES

HITTING AND STANDING HARD TOTALS

These strategies are applicable for single and multiple-deck games in all casino centers.

GENERAL PRINCIPLES

- When the dealer shows a 7, 8, 9, 10 or A, hit all hard totals of 16 or below (unless doubling or splitting is more profitable—in any case, you will always draw a card).
- When the dealer shows a 2, 3, 4, 5 or 6, stand on all hard totals of 12 or more. Do not bust against a dealer stiff card. Exception—Hit 12 versus 2, 3.

Reading the Charts

In all our charts, the dealer's upcard is indicated by the horizontal numbers, (running left to right) on the top row, and the player's hand is indicted by the vertical numbers (up and down) in the left column. The letters in the matrix indicate the correct strategy play.

HITTING AND STANDING—HARD TOTALS
All Casino Centers

		DEALER'S UPCARD									
		2	3	4	5	6	7	8	9	10	A
PLAYER'S HAND	11/less	H	H	H	H	H	H	H	H	H	H
	12	H	H	S	S	S	H	H	H	H	H
	13	S	S	S	S	S	H	H	H	H	H
	14	S	S	S	S	S	H	H	H	H	H
	15	S	S	S	S	S	H	H	H	H	H
	16	S	S	S	S	S	H	H	H	H	H
	17-21	S	S	S	S	S	S	S	S	S	S

H = Hit   S = Stand

CONCEPTUAL HITTING AND STANDING STRATEGY

In the "Understanding the Player's Hand" section, we discussed the strategy for hard totals of 11 or less, and for hard totals 17-21.

They will be reiterated briefly here.

- 11 or less—Draw against all dealer upcards.
- 17-21—Stand against all dealer upcards.

HARD TOTALS 12-16

It is when we hold hard totals 12-16, stiffs, that our big disadvantage of having to go first (the only built-in house advantage) is a costly proposition. If we draw to hard totals and bust, we are automatic losers. But, on the other hand, if we stand, we will win with these weak totals only when the dealer busts.

It is important to realize that the decision to hit or stand with hard totals 12-16 is a strategy of minimizing losses, for no matter what we do, we have a potentially losing hand against any dealer upcard. Do not expect to win when you hold a stiff. However, in order to maximize the gain from our overall strategy, we must minimize the losses in disadvantageous situations (as above), and maximize our gains in advantageous ones.

A. Player Totals of 12-16 Versus Dealer Pat Cards—7, 8, 9, 10, A

When the dealer's upcard is a 7 through an ace, you should expect the dealer to make his hand for he will bust only about one time in four, a mere 25% of the time. If we stand on our hard totals 12-16, we will win only the times that the dealer busts.

Thus, for every 100 hands that we stand with our stiff totals 12-16 against dealer pat cards, our expectation is to lose 75 of those hands and to win only 25, a net loss of 50 hands. Not an exciting prognosis.

On the other hand, drawing to our stiff totals 12-16 against the dealer pat cards gives us a big gain over standing. By drawing, we will gain an average of 15%. The dealer makes too many hands showing a 7, 8, 9, 10 or ace, to allow us to stand with our stiffs.

You will bust often when drawing to your stiffs, but do not let that dissuade you from hitting your stiffs against the dealer's pat cards. The strategy on these plays is to minimize losses. We cannot afford to stand and sacrifice our bet to the three out of four hands that the dealer will make.

When the dealer shows a 7, 8, 9, 10, or ace, hit all hard totals 16 or below.

B. Player Totals of 12-16 Versus Dealer Stiff Cards—2, 3, 4, 5, 6

The greater busting potential of the dealer stiff cards makes standing with hard player totals of 12-16 a big gain over drawing. While we will win only 40% of these hands (the times that the dealer busts), standing is a far superior strategy to drawing. We will bust too often drawing to our own stiffs against upcards that will bust fairly often themselves. The times that we would make pat totals by drawing wouldn't guarantee us winners either, for the dealer will often make equal or better totals.

On these plays, our disadvantage of having to go first makes drawing too costly, for once we bust, we automatically lose. Though the dealer will make more hands than bust, our strategy here is to minimize losses so that when we get our good hands, we'll come out an overall winner.

EXCEPTION—HIT PLAYER 12 VERSUS 2 OR 3

Hitting 12 versus 2, 3 is the only basic strategy exception to drawing with a stiff total against a dealer's stiff upcard. The double bust factor is not as costly on these plays for only the tens will bust our 12. Similarly, the dealer will bust less often showing a 2 or a 3 than with the other stiff cards, 4, 5 and 6.

This is in contrast to the play 13 versus 2 where the correct strategy is to stand. The additional player busting factor of the 9 makes it slightly better off to stand, even though the dealer will bust less with a 2 as an upcard. This clearly illustrates the greater importance of the player's busting factor (compared to the dealer's busting factor) when deciding whether to stand or draw with a stiff total 12-16 versus a dealer stiff upcard.

The combination of the player being less likely to bust (more likely to make his hand) and the dealer being more likely to make his hand (less likely to bust) makes drawing 12 versus 2 or 3 the correct strategy play.

HITTING AND STANDING SOFT TOTALS

The strategy for hitting and standing with soft totals in Northern Nevada and Europe is identical to the Atlantic City and Las Vegas strategies for both single and multiple deck, except that the Atlantic City and Las Vegas basic strategy players can take advantage of the more liberal doubling rules.

As a result, they will double down on hands that bettors playing Northern Nevada and European Style rules cannot.

HITTING AND STANDING—SOFT TOTALS Northern Nevada & Europe Single & Multiple Decks										
	DEALER'S UPCARD									
	2	3	4	5	6	7	8	9	10	A
A2-A6	H	H	H	H	H	H	H	H	H	H
A7	S	S	S	S	S	S	S	H	H	H
A8-A9	S	S	S	S	S	S	S	S	S	S
H = Hit S = Stand										

This next chart shows the Basic Strategy plays for hitting and standing with soft totals in Atlantic City and Las Vegas. Doubling strategies, which will be covered later, are also shown.

HITTING AND STANDING–SOFT TOTALS
Atlantic City & Las Vegas
Single & Multiple Decks

		DEALER'S UPCARD									
		2	3	4	5	6	7	8	9	10	A
PLAYER'S HAND	A2-A5	H	H	D*	D	D	H	H	H	H	H
	A6	D**	D	D	D	D	H	H	H	H	H
	A7	S	D	D	D	D	S	S	H	H	H
	A8	S	S	S	S	S	S	S	S	S	S
	A9	S	S	S	S	S	S	S	S	S	S

H = Hit   S = Stand   D = Double

* Do not double A2 versus 4 and A3 versus 4 in a multiple-deck game.

** Do not double A6 versus 2 in a multiple-deck game.

CONCEPTUAL HITTING AND STANDING–SOFT TOTALS

Player's Hand of A2, A3, A4, A5

Unless you are able to double down, you should always draw a card to these hands. Standing is a poor option, for these totals will win only when the dealer busts. You have nothing to lose by drawing (no draw can bust these totals), and a good card may improve your total. Players that stand on these hands might just as well give the casinos their money.

Draw on A2-A5 against all dealer upcards.

Player's Hand of A6, A7, A8, A9

The decision to hit or stand with soft totals 17 or higher necessitates a closer look at the strength of these totals. Unlike hard totals of 17 or more, drawing is a viable option with these soft totals. Since we have the option of counting the ace as 1 point or 11 points, the drawing of a 10, or for that matter, the drawing of any other card, will not bust our soft totals.

While we have no risk of busting, we do have the risk of drawing a weaker total, and therefore must ask the question, "How strong is our total?"

For soft totals, we want to know:

- What are our chances of winning by standing?
- What are the chances of improving our hand by drawing additional cards?

Player's Hand of Soft 17 (A6)

A standing total of 17 is a weak hand against all dealer upcards, including the dealer stiff cards, and in the long run is a loser. The only time we will win with this total is when the dealer busts. Otherwise, at best we have a push.

Always draw on soft 17 no matter what the dealer shows as an upcard. (In Las Vegas, Atlantic City and other locations where allowed, the correct strategy may be to double down. See "doubling down" section.) This standing total is so weak that attempting to improve our hand by drawing is always a tremendous gain against any upcard.

When a casino requires the dealer to draw to soft 17, it is a disadvantageous rule to you. Though the dealer will sometimes bust by drawing to a soft 17, in the long run he will make more powerful totals and have more winners. It affects us the same way.

Player's Hand of Soft 18

Against dealer stiff totals of 2, 3, 4, 5 and 6, standing with our 18 is a smart strategy move (unless playing Las Vegas or Atlantic City doubling rules where doubling will often be a big player gain). We have a strong total against these weak dealer upcards.

Stand against dealer upcards of 7 and 8, for our 18 is a solid hand. Against the 7, we have a winning total, and against the 8, we figure to have a potential push, as these dealer upcards gravitate toward 17 and 18 respectively. We do not want to risk our strong position by drawing.

Against the powerful dealer upcards of 9, 10, ace, our standing total of 18 is a potentially losing hand. Normally, you might think that hitting a soft 18 is a terrible play, however, 18 is not that strong. We are not chancing a powerful total but rather attempting to improve a weak situation.

As a matter of fact, for every 100 plays (at $1 a play) that we draw rather than stand on soft 18 versus 9 and 10, we will gain $9 and $4 respectively. That's a substantial gain. You must realize that 18 versus 9, 10, or ace is not a winning hand and since our 18 is a soft total, we have a chance to minimize losses by drawing.

Player's Hand of Soft 19 and 20

These hands are strong player totals as they stand. Do not draw any cards. We have no need of improving these already powerful totals.

DOUBLING DOWN

Doubling down is a valuable option for it gives you a chance to double your bet in advantageous situations. The only drawback to the doubling option is that you receive one card, giving up the privilege to draw additional ones should that card be a poor draw.

To determine if the doubling option will be profitable, we must weigh the benefits of doubling our bet against the drawbacks of receiving only one card.

One of the most important factors to consider when contemplating the doubling option is the ten factor. We are more likely to draw a 10 on our double than any other card value. Thus, doubling on a total of 11, where the drawing of a

10 gives us an unbeatable 21, is a more powerful double than an initial two-card total of 9, where the drawing of 10 gives us a strong total of 19, not nearly as powerful as the 21.

On the other hand, we would not double any hand of hard 12 or more, for the drawing of a 10 would bust our hand, and we would have an automatic loser at double the bet.

The ten factor is also an important strategic consideration, for it affects the dealer's busting potential. The more likely a dealer is to bust, the more doubling plays we will make. We double more aggressively against the weakest of the dealer stiff cards, the 4, 5 and 6, and less aggressively against the other stiff cards, the 2 and 3.

The only times we will double against the dealer pat cards are when our doubling totals of 10 and 11, hands that could turn into 20s and 21s, are powerful themselves.

SINGLE DECK DOUBLING STRATEGY

A. Northern Nevada Single Deck Doubling

You are restricted to doubling down on two-card totals of 10 and 11 only.

SINGLE DECK DOUBLING DOWN Northern Nevada										
	DEALER'S UPCARD									
PLAYER'S HAND	2	3	4	5	6	7	8	9	10	A
10	D	D	D	D	D	D	D	D		
11	D	D	D	D	D	D	D	D	D	D

D = Double Down   Blank = Hit, Do Not Double Down

B. Las Vegas— Single Deck Doubling

You may double down on any initial two-card combination.

SINGLE DECK DOUBLING DOWN Las Vegas											
		DEALER'S UPCARD									
		2	3	4	5	6	7	8	9	10	A
	62										
	44/53				D	D					
	9	D	D	D	D	D					
	10	D	D	D	D	D	D	D	D		
	11	D	D	D	D	D	D	D	D	D	D
	A2			D	D	D					
	A3			D	D	D					
	A4			D	D	D					
	A5			D	D	D					
	A6	D	D	D	D	D					
	A7		D	D	D	D					
	A8										
	A9										

D = Double Down   Blank = Hit, Do Not Double Down

MULTIPLE DECK DOUBLING STRATEGY

You'll notice that the doubling strategies for multiple-deck play are somewhat less aggressive than the single-deck game, a difference we'll discuss a little later on.

First we'll discuss Northern Nevada, where there are three changes from single-deck play, then Atlantic City and Las Vegas, where there are seven differences, and finally, European style, where there are five differences in doubling strategy from single-deck play.

However, only concern yourself now with the proper play for the games you'll face, and when you encounter different conditions and rules, then make the slight adjustments necessary for that game.

A. Northern Nevada—
Multiple Deck Doubling

You may double down on two-card totals of 10 and 11 only.

	MULTIPLE DECK DOUBLING DOWN Northern Nevada									
		DEALER'S UPCARD								
		2	3	4	5	6	7	8	9	10	A
PLAYER'S HAND	10	D	D	D	D	D	D	D	D		
	11	D	D	D	D	D	D	D	D	D	

D = Double Down   Blank = Hit, Do Not Double Down

B. Las Vegas, Atlantic City— Multiple Deck Doubling

You can double down on any initial two-card combination. These strategies are valid for all multiple-deck games in Atlantic City and Las Vegas.

		MULTIPLE DECK DOUBLING DOWN Las Vegas & Atlantic City								
		DEALER'S UPCARD								
		2	3	4	5	6	7	8	9	10	A
P L A Y E R ' S H A N D	8										
	9		D	D	D	D					
	10	D	D	D	D	D	D	D	D		
	11	D	D	D	D	D	D	D	D	D	
	A2				D	D					
	A3				D	D					
	A4			D	D	D					
	A5			D	D	D					
	A6		D	D	D	D					
	A7		D	D	D	D					
	A8										
	A9										

D = Double Down   Blank = Do Not Double Down

C. European Style—
Multiple Deck Doubling Down

You may double down on totals of 9, 10 and 11 only. Due to the no-hole-card rules, you double down less aggressively with these rules against the dealer's 10 than in Atlantic City and Nevada games as you can see in the following chart.

MULTIPLE DECK DOUBLING DOWN European Style Rules										
	DEALER'S UPCARD									
	2	3	4	5	6	7	8	9	10	A
9		D	D	D	D					
10	D	D	D	D	D	D	D	D		
11	D	D	D	D	D	D	D	D		

D = Double Down   Blank = Do Not Double Down

CONCEPTUAL DOUBLING—
HARD TOTALS (11, 10, 9, 8)

These strategies are applicable to single and multiple-deck games in all casino centers. Where multiple deck strategies differ from the single deck, an asterisk will denote the strategy change, and that change will be indicated.

Doubling 11

This is the strongest doubling hand and should be doubled against all dealer upcards in a single-deck game.* If we draw a

* Do not double 11 versus ace in multiple-deck games. In no-hole-card games, hit, do not double against the 10 or ace.

10 on our double, we will have a 21, the strongest hand we can have. At best, the dealer can tie us.

Doubling 10

This is the second strongest doubling hand for the player and should be doubled against the dealer's 2 through 9. Our hard 10 gravitates toward a 20, an overwhelmingly strong hand against these dealer upcards.

Do not double 10 against the dealer's 10 or ace. Doubling our hard 10 against the dealer's 10 is not a potential winner against the dealer's 2 through 9 for the dealer's hand gravitates toward a 20 as well, and our potential 20 is not powerful enough to compensate for the low busting probabilities of the dealer's ace either. Giving up the option to draw an additional card should our first draw be weak is too costly on these plays.

Note: In Northern Nevada, only hard 10 and 11 can be doubled down.

Doubling 9

Double 9 against 2 through 6 only.* The high busting potential of the dealer stiff cards (2-6) makes the 9 a profitable double down. We cannot double down against any of the pat cards (7-ace) for our win potential when we do draw the 10 (for a total of 19) is not strong enough to compensate for the times when we draw a poor card and cannot draw again.

Doubling 8

Doubling 8 versus 5 or 6 is a valid play in a single-deck game.** Our 8 gravitates toward an 18, only a fair total. However, the very high busting potential of the dealer 5 and 6 make this double a slight gain. Our 8 is not strong enough to make doubling against the other dealer upcards a good play.

---

* Do not double 9 versus 2 in a multiple-deck game.

** Do not double 8 versus any upcard in a multiple-deck game.

CONCEPTUAL DOUBLING— SOFT TOTALS

The high concentration of tens play a different role in soft doubling than in hard doubling, for instead of having a positive effect on our chances of making a good total, the drawing of a 10 will not even give us a pat hand on many of these situations.

Doubling with soft totals is generally a gain against weak dealer upcards. The ten factor figures strongly in the dealer's chances of busting, while on the other hand, the drawing of small and medium cards will often improve our hand to a competitive and winning total.

Doubling A2, A3, A4, A5

Double A2, A3, A4 and A5 against the dealer's 4, 5 and 6.*

The high busting probabilities of the dealer 4, 5 and 6 makes doubling with our A2 to A5 a profitable play. Again, the drawing of a 10-value card does not help our total, but the high dealer busting factor gives us an edge.

We do not double against the 2 or 3, because the dealer makes too many hands with these upcards. The same is more strikingly true with the dealer pat cards, 7 through ace.

Doubling A6

Double A6 versus dealer 2, 3, 4, 5 and 6.** The A6 is a more powerful double than the A2-A5, for the drawing of a 10 to the A6 will at least give us a pat total and a potential push against a dealer's 17. This "push factor" enables us to gain by doubling against the dealer's 2 and 3 despite the fact that they will make more dealer pat totals than with the weaker upcards 4, 5 and 6.

---

* Do not double A2 or A3 versus 4 in a multiple-deck game.

** Do not double A6 versus 2 in a multiple-deck game.

Doubling A7

Double A7 versus 3, 4, 5 and 6. Our soft 18 is only a fair total and drawing an additional card won't risk the destruction of a powerful total such as a 19 or 20.

Soft 18 is a strong double against the weaker dealer stiffs 4, 5 and 6, but differs from the soft 17 in that we do not double against the 2. A standing total of 18 versus a 2 is a stronger winning hand and we do not want to risk its weakening by doubling and having to draw a card.

Doubling A8, A9

We have two very strong totals here and do not want to risk our excellent chances of winning by attempting to double.

Stand with these powerful hands—do not double.

SPLITTING PAIRS

Splitting can do two valuable things. It can turn one poor total into two stronger hands, such as splitting a hard 16 (8-8) into two hands of 8 each, and it effectively doubles our bet.

The decision to split requires a closer look at our hand versus the dealer's hand. To come to the right decision, we must balance the standing total of our hand against the two proposed split hands and see if the split and resultant doubling of our bet increases our expectation of winning.

Here's our thought process:

- **How strong is our total as it stands?**
  Is the hand too powerful a total as it stands to risk breaking up? If not, we can consider the split.

- **How strong are the two proposed split totals?**
  Thinking in terms of the ten factor, we want to see if our split hands gravitate toward strong totals relative to

the strength of the dealer's upcard, or if the split totals represent an improvement over the original hand.

• **Does splitting either increase our chances of winning or reduce our rate of loss?**
Obviously, this is an important factor as well.

SPLITTING PAIRS—
SINGLE DECK BASIC STRATEGY

These strategies are applicable to all Northern Nevada and Las Vegas single-deck games.

	SINGLE DECK SPLITTING PAIRS Northern Nevada & Las Vegas									
	DEALER'S UPCARD									
	2	3	4	5	6	7	8	9	10	A
22		spl	spl	spl	spl	spl				
33			spl	spl	spl	spl				
44										
55										
66	spl	spl	spl	spl	spl					
77	spl	spl	spl	spl	spl	spl				
88	spl	spl	spl	spl	spl	spl	spl	spl	spl	spl
99	spl	spl	spl	spl	spl		spl	spl		
1010										
AA	spl	spl	spl	spl	spl	spl	spl	spl	spl	spl

spl = Split   Blank = Do Not Split

Do not split 44, 55, 10 10   Always split 88, AA

SPLITTING PAIRS—
MULTIPLE DECK BASIC STRATEGY

We will split slightly less aggressively against a multiple-deck game than against a single-deck game especially when the game is played with the no-hole-card rules. On the other hand, when the game offers doubling after splitting, we get more aggressive.

What happens when a multiple-deck game offers doubling after splitting?

We'll cover each of the possibilities in turn, showing you the best way to play no matter the situation.

A. Las Vegas and N. Nevada
Multiple Deck Splitting

The standard game allows pair splitting on any two cards but does not allow doubling after splitting. (If the particular game allows doubling after splitting, use the Atlantic City chart.)

		2	3	4	5	6	7	8	9	10	A
	22			spl	spl	spl	spl				
	33			spl	spl	spl	spl				
	44										
	55										
	66		spl	spl	spl	spl					
	77	spl	spl	spl	spl	spl	spl				
	88	spl	spl	spl	spl	spl	spl	spl	spl	spl	spl
	99	spl	spl	spl	spl	spl		spl	spl		
	1010										
	AA	spl	spl	spl	spl	spl	spl	spl	spl	spl	spl

MULTIPLE DECK SPLITTING PAIRS — Northern Nevada & Las Vegas — DEALER'S UPCARD — PLAYER'S HAND

spl = Split   Blank = Do Not Split

Do not split 44, 55, 10 10 Always Split 88, AA

B. Atlantic City Multiple Deck Splitting (and Nevada casinos that offer doubling down after splitting)

Because of the doubling after splitting rule, you will split pairs more aggressively so that you can take advantage of good doubling situations that may arise as a consequence of the split.

MULTIPLE DECK SPLITTING PAIRS Atlantic City										
	DEALER'S UPCARD									
	2	3	4	5	6	7	8	9	10	A
22	spl	spl	spl	spl	spl	spl				
33	spl	spl	spl	spl	spl	spl				
44				spl	spl					
55										
66	spl	spl	spl	spl	spl					
77	spl	spl	spl	spl	spl	spl				
88	spl	spl	spl	spl	spl	spl	spl	spl	spl	spl
99	spl	spl	spl	spl	spl		spl	spl		
1010										
AA	spl	spl	spl	spl	spl	spl	spl	spl	spl	spl

spl = Split   Blank = Do Not Split

Do not split 55, 10 10   Always split 88, AA

C. European Style Splitting

You will split less aggressively than the Atlantic City (and certainly the Nevada) casinos due to the no-hole-card rule. This chart assumes that doubling after splitting is not allowed.

		2	3	4	5	6	7	8	9	10	A
		MULTIPLE DECK SPLITTING PAIRS European Style Rules									
		DEALER'S UPCARD									
	22			spl	spl	spl	spl				
	33			spl	spl	spl	spl				
	44										
	55										
	66		spl	spl	spl	spl					
	77	spl	spl	spl	spl	spl	spl				
	88	spl	spl	spl	spl	spl	spl	spl	spl		
	99	spl	spl	spl	spl	spl		spl	spl		
	1010										
	AA	spl	spl	spl	spl	spl	spl	spl	spl	spl	

spl = Split   Blank = Do Not Split

Do not split 44, 55, 10 10

D. European Style—Doubling After Splitting Allowed

Many international casinos allow doubling after splitting. When this option is available, you will take advantage of it by splitting more aggressively.

SPLITTING PAIRS
DOUBLING AFTER SPLITTING ALLOWED
European Style Rules

PLAYER'S HAND		DEALER'S UPCARD									
		2	3	4	5	6	7	8	9	10	A
	22	spl	spl	spl	spl	spl	spl				
	33	spl	spl	spl	spl	spl	spl				
	44				spl	spl					
	55										
	66	spl	spl	spl	spl	spl					
	77	spl	spl	spl	spl	spl	spl				
	88	spl	spl	spl	spl	spl	spl	spl	spl		
	99	spl	spl	spl	spl	spl		spl	spl		
	1010										
	AA	spl	spl	spl	spl	spl	spl	spl	spl	spl	

spl = Split   Blank = Do Not Split

Do not split 55, 10 10

CONCEPTUAL SPLITTING

We will examine the decision to split 99 first, for it is a good example of the thinking process involved in splitting. First of all, we should note that this hand totaling 18 is only "fair," not a powerful total like a 19 or 20.

Splitting 99—Dealer shows a 2, 3, 4, 5, 6

Split 99 against these dealer stiff cards. Our 18 is a winner, but splitting the hand into two halves of 9 each is a big gain. Each starting hand of 9, because of the ten factor, gravitates toward strong player totals of 19.

The high busting potential of the dealer stiff cards gives us an excellent opportunity to maximize our gain in an advantageous situation.

Splitting 99—Dealer shows a 7

Stand with 99 versus dealer 7. We figure the dealer for a 17. Our standing total of 18 is a stronger total and a big potential winner. While splitting 9s will also produce a positive expectation of winning, the risking of our fairly secure 18 against the 7 for two strong but speculative totals reduces the gain.

We have the dealer beat. Stand.

Splitting 99—Dealer shows an 8

Splitting 99 against the dealer's 8 is a big gain.

Against the dealer's 8, we figure our 18 to be a potential push. However, by splitting the 18 into two separate hands of 9 each, we hope to turn our potential push into two possible winners. (Each 9 gravitates toward a total of 19, one point higher than the dealer's 18.)

Splitting 99—Dealer shows a 9

Splitting 99 versus the dealer's 9 is also a big gain.

Against the 9, our 18 is a losing total, but splitting the 18 into two totals of 9 each reduces our potential loss. Rather than one losing total of 18, we will have two hands gravitating toward potential pushes.

Splitting 99—Dealer shows a 10 or ace

Do not split 99 against the dealer's 10 or ace.

Our split hands of 9 each gravitate toward good totals, but against these more powerful dealer upcards, splitting would be a poor play. We do not want to make one loser into two.

The correct play is to draw the 99 against the 10 or ace.

Splitting 22 and 33

Split 22 versus dealer 3 through 7*

Split 33 versus dealer 4 through 7**

The high busting probabilities of the dealer 4, 5 and 6 makes the 22 and 33 good splits. We split 22 versus 3 and not 33 versus 3, because of the lower player busting factor of our split hands of 2 each. The drawing of a 10 gives us another chance to improve on our hand, for correct basic strategy is to draw 12 versus 3, while the drawing of a 10 on our 3 forces us to stand.

We do not split 22 or 33 versus the dealer's 2, because the dealer's 2 does not bust often enough to make splitting a profitable play.

Splitting 22 and 33 versus 7 seems unusual at first, for this play seems to exceed our normal strategic boundaries of making aggressive plays against the weak dealer stiff cards. Though the 7 is a pat card and will make a lot of pat hands, the 7 will also make the weakest totals, only gravitating toward a total of 17. Our starting totals of 2 and 3 will make hands of 18 or better about one-half the time. Splitting 22 and 33 against the dealer's 7 will not make us money (because of the high busting factor of our hands), but they will produce a moderate gain over drawing to these hands.

Do not split 22 and 33 against the 8, 9, 10 or ace. We do not want to make one loser into two losers.

---

* Nevada multiple deck exception—Do not split 22 versus 3.

** Atlantic City multiple deck exception (and games with doubling after splitting allowed)—split 22 and 33 versus 2 through 7.

Splitting 44

Do not split 44.* The hard total of 8 gravitates toward a total of 18, a far better position than two weak starting totals of 4 each. Against the dealer stiff cards, 2 through 6, we have a big gain by drawing to our 8. While the drawing of a 10 will not give us an overwhelmingly strong total, an 18 is far better than drawing the same 10 to a split 4.

We do not want to hold two weak hands of 4 each against the dealer pat cards, especially the dealer's 7 and 8, where we already have a competitive starting total of 8.

Splitting 55

Never split 55. 55 by itself is an excellent starting total of 10. You do not want to break up this powerful player total into two terrible hands of 5 each. (Our 10 is an excellent doubling hand against dealer upcards of 2 through 9.)

Splitting 66

Split 66 against dealer stiff cards 2 through 6 only.** Our hard total of 12 is not very favorable, nor are the split hands of 6 and 6 too promising either. We have a losing hand either way against all dealer upcards. However, we want to minimize our losses.

Against the dealer stiff cards 2, 3, 4, 5 and 6, our split hands of 6 and 6 will sometimes draw cards to give us some pat totals 17-21.

Of course, we will often end up with stiff totals on the split pair (by the drawing of a 10 or other large card) and be forced

---

* Atlantic City exception (and games with doubling after splitting allowed)—Split 44 versus 5 and 6. The added possibilities of being able to double our bet should either or both of the split totals pull well makes this split an advantageous move.

** Nevada multiple deck exception—Do not split 66 versus 2.
Atlantic City multiple deck (and games with doubling after splitting allowed)—no exceptions; split 66 versus 2-6.

to stand. But the high dealer busting factor makes splitting 66 against the dealer stiffs a slight gain.

Obviously we will not split 66 against the dealer pat cards. We don't need two hands of 16 against a card that will bust only one time in four.

Splitting 77

Split 77 against dealer upcards of 2, 3, 4, 5, 6 and 7. Against the dealer stiff cards 2 through 6, two playable hands of 7 and 7 are preferable to one stiff total of 14. Splitting 77 is not a strong split, for these totals only gravitate toward a 17, but the high busting rate of the dealer stiff cards makes this split a big gain.

Splitting 77 against the dealer's 7 is also an excellent split, for we are taking one losing total of 14 into two potential pushes of 17 each.

We do not split 77 versus the dealer's 8, 9, 10 and ace, for we do not want to take one poor total of 14 into two hands gravitating toward a second-best total of only 17.

Splitting 88

Split 88 against all dealer upcards. Against the dealer's 2 through 8, we are taking one terrible hand of 16 into two playable totals of 8 each. There is a tremendous gain on all these plays.

Splitting 88 against the dealer's 9, 10, A are the strangest of the basic strategy plays. Using all of the intuitive knowledge we have developed, at first glance we would reason that this is a poor split, for we are making two losers out of one. However, more is involved in this play.

First, you must realize that the player hand of 16 is the worst total possible. While splitting this 16 into two hands of 8 and 8 is not a winning situation against the strong dealer upcards of 9, 10 and A, it is an improvement over our very weak total of hard 16.

Bear with this unusual play, for computer simulation studies have played out the hand millions of times for both drawing and splitting, and found that you lose less by splitting 88 against the dealer's 9, 10, or ace. Keep in mind that although the split is weak, it does produce a gain over drawing to our easily bustable 16.

In games employing the no-hole-card rule, do not split 8s against the dealer's 10 and ace. With the possibility of the dealer getting a blackjack, we don't need more money out on this hand. Hit instead.

Splitting 10,10

Do not split tens. The hard total of 20 is a winning hand against all dealer upcards. Splitting tens against any dealer upcard is a terrible play, for you are taking one "solid" winning hand into two good but uncertain wins. Too often, the splitting of tens will draw low cards, in effect destroying a great hand.

Splitting AA

Split AA against all dealer upcards. Each ace is a powerful starting total of 11 points. If we draw a 10, our 21 can't be beat. (Note: Drawing a 10 here is not a blackjack.) Splitting AA is a tremendous gain against all dealer upcards.

In no-hole-card rule games, we will not split aces when the dealer shows an ace. The high likelihood of the dealer getting a blackjack when he already has an ace is too costly for us to double our bet. Draw instead.

THE MASTER CHARTS

MASTER CHART - SINGLE DECK
Northern Nevada

PLAYER'S HAND	DEALER'S UPCARD									
	2	3	4	5	6	7	8	9	10	A
7/less	H	H	H	H	H	H	H	H	H	H
8	H	H	H	H	H	H	H	H	H	H
9	H	H	H	H	H	H	H	H	H	H
10	D	D	D	D	D	D	D	D	H	H
11	D	D	D	D	D	D	D	D	D	D
12	H	H	S	S	S	H	H	H	H	H
13	S	S	S	S	S	H	H	H	H	H
14	S	S	S	S	S	H	H	H	H	H
15	S	S	S	S	S	H	H	H	H	H
16	S	S	S	S	S	H	H	H	H	H
A2	H	H	H	H	H	H	H	H	H	H
A3	H	H	H	H	H	H	H	H	H	H
A4	H	H	H	H	H	H	H	H	H	H
A5	H	H	H	H	H	H	H	H	H	H
A6	H	H	H	H	H	H	H	H	H	H
A7	S	S	S	S	S	S	S	H	H	H
A8	S	S	S	S	S	S	S	S	S	S
A9	S	S	S	S	S	S	S	S	S	S
22	H	spl	spl	spl	spl	spl	H	H	H	H
33	H	H	spl	spl	spl	spl	H	H	H	H
44	H	H	H	H	H	H	H	H	H	H
55	D	D	D	D	D	D	D	D	H	H
66	spl	spl	spl	spl	spl	H	H	H	H	H
77	spl	spl	spl	spl	spl	spl	H	H	H	H
88	spl	spl	spl	spl	spl	spl	spl	spl	spl	spl
99	spl	spl	spl	spl	spl	S	spl	spl	S	S
1010	S	S	S	S	S	S	S	S	S	S
AA	spl	spl	spl	spl	spl	spl	spl	spl	spl	spl

H = Hit   S = Stand   D = Double   spl = Split

Do not split 44, 55 and 10 10
Always split 88 and AA

MASTER CHART - SINGLE DECK Las Vegas									
DEALER'S UPCARD									
2	3	4	5	6	7	8	9	10	A

PLAYER'S HAND

	2	3	4	5	6	7	8	9	10	A
7/less	H	H	H	H	H	H	H	H	H	H
62	H	H	H	H	H	H	H	H	H	H
53	H	H	H	D	D	H	H	H	H	H
9	D	D	D	D	D	H	H	H	H	H
10	D	D	D	D	D	D	D	D	H	H
11	D	D	D	D	D	D	D	D	D	D
12	H	H	S	S	S	H	H	H	H	H
13	S	S	S	S	S	H	H	H	H	H
14	S	S	S	S	S	H	H	H	H	H
15	S	S	S	S	S	H	H	H	H	H
16	S	S	S	S	S	H	H	H	H	H
A2	H	H	D	D	D	H	H	H	H	H
A3	H	H	D	D	D	H	H	H	H	H
A4	H	H	D	D	D	H	H	H	H	H
A5	H	H	D	D	D	H	H	H	H	H
A6	D	D	D	D	D	H	H	H	H	H
A7	S	D	D	D	D	S	S	H	H	H
A8	S	S	S	S	S	S	S	S	S	S
A9	S	S	S	S	S	S	S	S	S	S
22	H	spl	spl	spl	spl	spl	H	H	H	H
33	H	H	spl	spl	spl	spl	H	H	H	H
44	H	H	H	D	D	H	H	H	H	H
55	D	D	D	D	D	D	D	D	H	H
66	spl	spl	spl	spl	spl	H	H	H	H	H
77	spl	spl	spl	spl	spl	spl	H	H	H	H
88	spl	spl	spl	spl	spl	spl	spl	spl	spl	spl
99	spl	spl	spl	spl	spl	S	spl	spl	S	S
1010	S	S	S	S	S	S	S	S	S	S
AA	spl	spl	spl	spl	spl	spl	spl	spl	spl	spl

H = Hit   S = Stand   D = Double   spl = Split

Do not split 44, 55 and 10 10
Always split 88 and AA

SINGLE- AND MULTIPLE-DECK BLACKJACK DIFFERENCES

As we have seen, the main variations in strategy take place with our doubling and splitting strategies—moves which entail an increased wager on the hand. Let's now see just why the single- and multiple-deck blackjack games are slightly different.

The greater number of cards used in a multiple-deck game makes the removal of any particular card or cards less important for composition change purposes and, as a result, our doubling and splitting strategies are less aggressive.

For example, the removal of three cards (5,3,5) creates a favorable imbalance for the player in a single-deck game and makes a 53 double versus the dealer's 5 a profitable play. Not only will these cards be poor draws for the player's double, but they're three cards the dealer needs to improve his hand. The effective removal of these three cards gives you a better chance of drawing a 10 on your 8 and, at the same time, increases the dealer's chance of busting. Thus, in a single-deck game, 53 versus 5 is a favorable double.

However, the removal of these three cards are barely felt in a four-deck game. There are twenty-nine other 3s and 5s in a four-deck game as compared to only five in a single deck. Thus, not enough of a favorable imbalance has been created in the multiple-deck game, and the double down is not a correct play.

This lack of sensitivity to particular card removal accounts for nine strategy changes in the multiple-deck game compared to the preceding single deck master charts we just presented.

Except for the following nine changes in the doubling and splitting strategies, multiple deck basic strategy is identical to the single deck basic strategy.

STRATEGY CHANGES IN MULTIPLE-DECK GAMES

In a multiple-deck game:

- 1 Do not double hard 8 versus 5 — hit instead.
- 2 Do not double hard 8 versus 6 — hit instead.
- 3 Do not double hard 9 versus 2 — hit instead.
- 4 Do not double hard 11 versus ace — hit instead.
- 5 Do not double A2 versus 4 — hit instead.
- 6 Do not double A3 versus 4 — hit instead.
- 7 Do not double A6 versus 2 — hit instead.
- 8 Do not split 22 versus 3 — hit instead.
- 9 Do not split 66 versus 2 — hit instead.

MASTER CHART - MULTIPLE DECK
Northern Nevada

	DEALER'S UPCARD									
	2	3	4	5	6	7	8	9	10	A
7/less	H	H	H	H	H	H	H	H	H	H
8	H	H	H	H	H	H	H	H	H	H
9	H	H	H	H	H	H	H	H	H	H
10	D	D	D	D	D	D	D	D	H	H
11	D	D	D	D	D	D	D	D	D	H
12	H	H	S	S	S	H	H	H	H	H
13	S	S	S	S	S	H	H	H	H	H
14	S	S	S	S	S	H	H	H	H	H
15	S	S	S	S	S	H	H	H	H	H
16	S	S	S	S	S	H	H	H	H	H
A2	H	H	H	H	H	H	H	H	H	H
A3	H	H	H	H	H	H	H	H	H	H
A4	H	H	H	H	H	H	H	H	H	H
A5	H	H	H	H	H	H	H	H	H	H
A6	H	H	H	H	H	H	H	H	H	H
A7	S	S	S	S	S	S	S	H	H	H
A8	S	S	S	S	S	S	S	S	S	S
A9	S	S	S	S	S	S	S	S	S	S
22	H	H	spl	spl	spl	spl	H	H	H	H
33	H	H	spl	spl	spl	spl	H	H	H	H
44	H	H	H	H	H	H	H	H	H	H
55	D	D	D	D	D	D	D	D	H	H
66	H	spl	spl	spl	spl	H	H	H	H	H
77	spl	spl	spl	spl	spl	spl	H	H	H	H
88	spl	spl	spl	spl	spl	spl	spl	spl	spl	spl
99	spl	spl	spl	spl	spl	S	spl	spl	S	S
1010	S	S	S	S	S	S	S	S	S	S
AA	spl	spl	spl	spl	spl	spl	spl	spl	spl	spl

H = Hit   S = Stand   D = Double   spl = Split

PLAYER'S HAND

Do not split 44, 55 and 10 10
Always split 88 and AA

MASTER CHART - MULTIPLE DECK Las Vegas									
DEALER'S UPCARD									
2	3	4	5	6	7	8	9	10	A
7/less H	H	H	H	H	H	H	H	H	H
8 H	H	H	H	H	H	H	H	H	H
9 H	D	D	D	D	H	H	H	H	H
10 D	D	D	D	D	D	D	D	H	H
11 D	D	D	D	D	D	D	D	D	H
12 H	H	S	S	S	H	H	H	H	H
13 S	S	S	S	S	H	H	H	H	H
14 S	S	S	S	S	H	H	H	H	H
15 S	S	S	S	S	H	H	H	H	H
16 S	S	S	S	S	H	H	H	H	H
A2 H	H	H	D	D	H	H	H	H	H
A3 H	H	H	D	D	H	H	H	H	H
A4 H	H	D	D	D	H	H	H	H	H
A5 H	H	D	D	D	H	H	H	H	H
A6 H	D	D	D	D	H	H	H	H	H
A7 S	D	D	D	D	S	S	H	H	H
A8 S	S	S	S	S	S	S	S	S	S
A9 S	S	S	S	S	S	S	S	S	S
22 H	H	spl	spl	spl	spl	H	H	H	H
33 H	H	spl	spl	spl	spl	H	H	H	H
44 H	H	H	H	H	H	H	H	H	H
55 D	D	D	D	D	D	D	D	H	H
66 H	spl	spl	spl	spl	H	H	H	H	H
77 spl	spl	spl	spl	spl	spl	H	H	H	H
88 spl	spl	spl	spl	spl	spl	spl	spl	spl	spl
99 spl	spl	spl	spl	spl	S	spl	spl	S	S
1010 S	S	S	S	S	S	S	S	S	S
AA spl	spl	spl	spl	spl	spl	spl	spl	spl	spl

H = Hit   S = Stand   D = Double   spl = Split

Do not split 44, 55 and 10 10
Always split 88 and AA

ATLANTIC CITY MULTIPLE DECK

The blackjack games offered in Atlantic City differ from the Nevada games in several ways. For one thing, most Atlantic City games are dealt from either a 4-, 6- or 8-deck shoe. In recent years, though, single-deck games have become available, but with a caveat—blackjacks are paid off at 6 to 5, which makes it a terrible game (that rule costs you 1.39%) and the dealer hits on soft 17 (which costs you another .20%). You should avoid any game where blackjacks only pay off at 6 to 5 (as opposed to the standard 3 to 2).

Doubling allowed after splitting is standard in Atlantic City, as opposed to Nevada, where only a few casinos offer this option. Resplitting of pairs is now allowed in Atlantic City, which is a change from the past.

To protect against collusion between the player and the dealer, the dealer does not check his hole card for a blackjack (as is standard in Nevada) until all the players have finished playing out their hands. This casino safeguard does not affect the player's chances of winning, for if the dealer does indeed have a blackjack, any additional money you may have wagered on a doubled or split hand will be returned. Only the original bet is lost.

Another difference is that all player hands are dealt face up in Atlantic City. No casinos allow the player to physically handle the cards. The player must employ hand signals to convey his strategy intentions to the dealer.

The Atlantic City basic strategy is the same as Nevada multiple-deck strategy except for more frequent pair splitting due to the player being allowed to double after splits.

MASTER CHART - MULTIPLE DECK Atlantic City									
DEALER'S UPCARD									
2	3	4	5	6	7	8	9	10	A

PLAYER'S HAND	2	3	4	5	6	7	8	9	10	A
7/less	H	H	H	H	H	H	H	H	H	H
8	H	H	H	H	H	H	H	H	H	H
9	H	D	D	D	D	H	H	H	H	H
10	D	D	D	D	D	D	D	D	H	H
11	D	D	D	D	D	D	D	D	D	H
12	H	H	S	S	S	H	H	H	H	H
13	S	S	S	S	S	H	H	H	H	H
14	S	S	S	S	S	H	H	H	H	H
15	S	S	S	S	S	H	H	H	H	H
16	S	S	S	S	S	H	H	H	H	H
A2	H	H	H	D	D	H	H	H	H	H
A3	H	H	H	D	D	H	H	H	H	H
A4	H	H	D	D	D	H	H	H	H	H
A5	H	H	D	D	D	H	H	H	H	H
A6	H	D	D	D	D	H	H	H	H	H
A7	S	D	D	D	D	S	S	H	H	H
A8	S	S	S	S	S	S	S	S	S	S
A9	S	S	S	S	S	S	S	S	S	S
22	spl	spl	spl	spl	spl	spl	H	H	H	H
33	spl	spl	spl	spl	spl	spl	H	H	H	H
44	H	H	H	spl	spl	H	H	H	H	H
55	D	D	D	D	D	D	D	D	H	H
66	H	spl	spl	spl	spl	H	H	H	H	H
77	spl	spl	spl	spl	spl	spl	H	H	H	H
88	spl	spl	spl	spl	spl	spl	spl	spl	spl	spl
99	spl	spl	spl	spl	spl	S	spl	spl	S	S
1010	S	S	S	S	S	S	S	S	S	S
AA	spl	spl	spl	spl	spl	spl	spl	spl	spl	spl

H = Hit   S = Stand   D = Double   spl = Split

Do not split 55 and 10 10   Always split 88 and AA

EUROPEAN NO-HOLE-CARD RULES

These strategies are for multiple-deck play and take into account that players may only double on totals of 9, 10 and 11, and also will double and split less aggressively when the dealer shows a 10 or ace due to the no-hole-card rule.

In no-hole-card games that allow the player to double after splitting, you will split more aggressively to take advantage of this favorable option. We'll show those strategy plays in a master chart.

					DEALER'S UPCARD					
MASTER CHART - MULTIPLE DECK European No-Hole-Card Style										
	2	3	4	5	6	7	8	9	10	A
7/less	H	H	H	H	H	H	H	H	H	H
8	H	H	H	H	H	H	H	H	H	H
9	H	D	D	D	D	H	H	H	H	H
10	D	D	D	D	D	D	D	D	H	H
11	D	D	D	D	D	D	D	D	H	H
12	H	H	S	S	S	H	H	H	H	H
13	S	S	S	S	S	H	H	H	H	H
14	S	S	S	·S	S	H	H	H	H	H
15	S	S	S	S	S	H	H	H	H	H
16	S	S	S	S	S	H	H	H	H	H
A2	H	H	H	H	H	H	H	H	H	H
A3	H	H	H	H	H	H	H	H	H	H
A4	H	H	H	H	H	H	H	H	H	H
A5	H	H	H	H	H	H	H	H	H	H
A6	H	H	H	H	H	H	H	H	H	H
A7	S	S	S	S	S	S	S	H	H	H
A8	S	S	S	S	S	S	S	S	S	S
A9	S	S	S	S	S	S	S	S	S	S
22	H	H	spl	spl	spl	spl	H	H	H	H
33	H	H	spl	spl	spl	spl	H	H	H	H
44	H	H	H	H	H	H	H	H	H	H
55	D	D	D	D	D	D	D	D	H	H
66	H	spl	spl	spl	spl	H	H	H	H	H
77	spl	spl	spl	spl	spl	spl	H	H	H	H
88	spl	spl	spl	spl	spl	spl	spl	spl	H	H
99	spl	spl	spl	spl	spl	S	spl	spl	S	S
1010	S	S	S	S	S	S	S	S	S	S
AA	spl	spl	spl	spl	spl	spl	spl	spl	spl	H
H = Hit S = Stand D = Double spl = Split										

PLAYER'S HAND

Do not split 44, 55 and 10 10

MASTER CHART - MULTIPLE DECK
European No-Hole-Card Style
Doubling After Splitting Allowed

	DEALER'S UPCARD									
	2	3	4	5	6	7	8	9	10	A
7/less	H	H	H	H	H	H	H	H	H	H
8	H	H	H	H	H	H	H	H	H	H
9	H	D	D	D	D	H	H	H	H	H
10	D	D	D	D	D	D	D	D	H	H
11	D	D	D	D	D	D	D	D	H	H
12	H	H	S	S	S	H	H	H	H	H
13	S	S	S	S	S	H	H	H	H	H
14	S	S	S	S	S	H	H	H	H	H
15	S	S	S	S	S	H	H	H	H	H
16	S	S	S	S	S	H	H	H	H	H
A2	H	H	H	H	H	H	H	H	H	H
A3	H	H	H	H	H	H	H	H	H	H
A4	H	H	H	H	H	H	H	H	H	H
A5	H	H	H	H	H	H	H	H	H	H
A6	H	H	H	H	H	H	H	H	H	H
A7	S	S	S	S	S	S	S	H	H	H
A8	S	S	S	S	S	S	S	S	S	S
A9	S	S	S	S	S	S	S	S	S	S
22	spl	spl	spl	spl	spl	spl	H	H	H	H
33	spl	spl	spl	spl	spl	spl	H	H	H	H
44	H	H	H	spl	spl	H	H	H	H	H
55	D	D	D	D	D	D	D	D	H	H
66	spl	spl	spl	spl	spl	H	H	H	H	H
77	spl	spl	spl	spl	spl	spl	H	H	H	H
88	spl .	spl	spl	spl	spl	spl	spl	spl	H	H
99	spl	spl	spl	spl	spl	S	spl	spl	S	S
1010	S	S	S	S	S	S	S	S	S	S
AA	spl	spl	spl	spl	spl	spl	spl	spl	spl	H

H = Hit   S = Stand   D = Double   spl = Split

Do not split 55 and 10 10

PLAYER'S OPTIONS

Use these strategies where the following options are permitted:

Doubling Down Permitted After Splitting

Doubling down after splitting is a standard option in Atlantic City, Great Britain and many casinos around the world, but offered only in a few Nevada casinos. This option allows the player to double down on one or more of the hands resulting from a split according to the standard doubling rules of the casino.

When doubling after splitting is permitted, we will split our pairs more aggressively to take advantage of good doubling situations that can arise as a consequence of the split. This option is favorable to the player.

DOUBLING DOWN PERMITTED AFTER SPLITTING			
Player's Hand		Single Deck	Multiple Deck
22	split against	2-7	2-7
33	split against	2-7	2-7
44	split against	4-6	5-6
66	split against	2-7	2-6
77	split against	2-8	2-7

Late Surrender

Late surrender is a player option to forfeit your hand and lose half the bet *after* it has been determined that the dealer doesn't have a blackjack. In other words, if the dealer has a blackjack, you will lose your bet before you have a chance to surrender. This option is a favorable option for you.

LATE SURRENDER			
Player's Hand		**Single Deck**	**Multiple Deck**
16*	surrender against	10, A	9, 10, A
15	surrender against	10	10
77	surrender against	10	-

Do not surrender soft totals   * Do not surrender 88 (split)

Early Surrender

A player option to forfeit his hand and lose half his bet *before* the dealer checks for a blackjack. A rare option, but extremely valuable for the player if available because you're able to surrender your cards and save half your bet even though the dealer may have a blackjack.

EARLY SURRENDER SINGLE AND MULTIPLE DECK GAMES		
Dealer's Upcard		**Player's Totals**
A	early surrender with	5-7, 12-17
10	early surrender with	14-16
9	early surrender with	16*

Do not surrender soft totals   *Do not early surrender 88 (split)

THE WINNING EDGE

The removal of cards from play and the continued dealing from a deck depleted of these played cards creates situations in blackjack where the odds of receiving particular cards or combinations of cards constantly change. Computer studies have found that the proportionate removal of certain cards gives the player an advantage over the house, while the proportionate removal of others gives the house an advantage over the player.

Thus, as cards are removed from play, the player's chances of winning constantly change. Sometimes the depleted deck of cards will favor the house and sometimes the player. By learning to analyze a depleted deck of cards for favorability, and capitalizing on particular situations by betting more when the remaining cards are in your favor and less when they're not in your favor, you can actually have an edge over the casino.

The heart of all winning systems at blackjack is based on this theory—betting more when you have the advantage, and less when the house has the advantage. This way, when you win, you win more, and when you lose, you lose less. Beginning with an even game (playing accurate basic strategy), this "maximize gain, minimize loss" betting strategy will give you an overall edge on the house.

How do we determine when we have the edge?

UNDERSTANDING THE VALUE OF CARDS

Tens and aces are the most valuable cards for the player, while the small cards, 2s through 7s, are the most valuable cards for the house, 8s and 9s being relatively neutral. Off the top of the deck, with all cards still in play, you have an even game with the house—neither side enjoys an advantage.* The odds shift in your favor when there is a higher ratio of tens and aces in the deck than normal, and shift in favor of the house when there is a higher ratio of small cards, 2s through 7s, than normal.

All counting systems base their winning strategies on keeping track of the ratio of high cards to low cards. The systems vary in complexity from the very simple to the very complicated, all being based on the same principle—betting more when there is a higher proportion of tens and aces in the deck, and less when there is a higher proportion of low cards, 2s through 7s, remaining.

However, there are many blackjack players who wish to have an edge over the house but are loathe to learn counting systems. For the player that desires to win without counting cards, the Cardoza School of Blackjack has developed some simple but effective techniques.

THE CARDOZA NON-COUNTER STRATEGY—FIVE EASY STEPS

The system is simple. All you need to know is that high cards favor us and small cards favor the house.

When there are more high cards in the deck than normal, you will bet more.

---

* Assuming the player plays perfect basic strategy as we've shown, and that the game is a single-deck game with the favorable Las Vegas Strip rules. If the particular game has less liberal rules (Northern Nevada) or is a multiple-deck game, the house enjoys a slight initial edge.

But you need not count cards. All you need to do is to keep your eyes open and watch the cards, just as you probably do anyway.

Five easy guidelines for non-counters to enjoy an edge over the casino:

1. When many small cards have been played in the first round, it is to the player's advantage. Bet 3 or 4 units instead of your normal 1 or 2 unit bet. If $5 is your standard bet, then $15 is considered a 3 unit bet; and if $25 is your standard bet, then your 3 unit bet would be $75.

   Let's look at an example. We're dealt 8, 5, 6; the player to your left had 10, 6, 2; another player had 10, 6, 5; and the dealer had a 9, 7. A disproportionate number of small cards have been played, meaning the remaining cards are richer in high cards—to the player's advantage. So you bet more.

2. If, on succeeding rounds, you estimate that there are still a disproportionate number of high cards remaining, continue to bet at a higher level than your minimum or neutral bet. Through practical experience, you will be able to improve on your estimation abilities.

3. If the cumulative distribution of cards seems to be fairly normal after a round of play, bet your neutral or minimum bet (1 or 2 units, whatever your preference). If, however, you notice that no aces have appeared, increase your bet by one unit. Your potential to get a blackjack has increased. While the dealer's chances of getting a blackjack has increased as well, he only gets paid even-money; you get paid 3 to 2 (or 6 to 5).

4. On the other hand, if a disproportionate number of high cards appear in the first round, then place your minimum 1 unit bet, for the house has an edge. If, on succeeding rounds, you judge that there is still a disproportionate number of small cards remaining, continue to place your minimum bets.

5. If the cumulative distribution of cards appears to be normal and you notice that more aces have appeared than what you normally would expect (one ace for every 13 cards is the normal composition), you want to downgrade your bet to 1 unit if you had been making 2 unit bets.

QUICK SUMMARY OF THE FIVE WINNING PRINCIPLES

When there are more tens and aces remaining in the deck than normal, increase your bet. When there are fewer tens and aces than normal (meaning more small cards), decrease your bet. Every time the deck is shuffled, start your estimation of favorability over again.

BET RANGE

I recommend a bet range of 1-4 units in a single-deck game. Thus, if $5 is your standard bet, your maximum bet should not exceed $20; if you're a $25 player, $100 should be the maximum. This is an important guideline to adhere to for the following five reasons:

1. Your advantage will rarely be large enough to warrant a bet larger than 4 units. We have bankroll limitations to consider, and do not want recklessness

to be our downfall. Keep in mind that winning blackjack is a slow grind for the good players.

2. Raising your bets in advantageous situations to a range greater than 1-4 will attract undue attention to you as a skillful player, and the casino may begin to shuffle every time you make a large bet, in effect shuffling away advantageous situations.

3. You do not want to have one extremely large losing bet destroy an otherwise good session at the table.

4. The losing of a disproportionately large bet can have a detrimental effect on your confidence, your concentration, and your ability to think clearly. You will be surprised at how fast this can affect your physical and psychological frame of being, and cause you to play poorly. That's why we limit the upper range of our bets to four times the size of the smallest bet.

5. The ranging of your bets from 1 unit in disadvantageous situations to 4 units in highly advantageous situations is a wide enough bet spread to maximize your gains while at the same time minimizing your risk.

THE POWER OF YOUR ADVANTAGE

The Cardoza Non-Counter strategy gives you an advantage powerful enough when betting $5 to $20 per hand for a $100 profit expectancy in a heavy weekend of play in a single-deck game. When betting $25 to $100 per hand as I suggest, you have a $500 expectancy of winning if you play a perfect Basic Strategy.

These profit expectations are realistic numbers you can reach based on those betting limits and not pie-in-the-sky numbers that will be life-changing. Of course, you could get hot and win five or ten times those amounts, though those kind of sessions will not come often. You could also get cold and lose hand after hand, but if you follow the money management advice in this book, you can never lose equal amounts to what you might win because you will quit and initiate damage control long before you ever get to unsightly amounts of losses.

The idea here is to play sanely and get the edge over the casino, grinding them out as opposed to them grinding you out. If you play them tough, you'll be feeling a whole lot better with wins in your pocket. It's always more enjoyable to be the winner than the loser, which, when you have the edge, will be more likely than players who play haphazardly and give percentages to the casino—something you as a winning player won't do.

The Cardoza Non-Counter strategy is most effective in single-deck games, and less so in double-deck ones due to the smaller number of cards. This strategy's main advantage is that it allows you to win with much less mental effort than counting systems require while having fun at the same time!

Now that you have the winning edge on the house, time will work to your advantage. The longer you play, the more money you can expect to make. Obviously you cannot win as much without counting cards, but you can still win—with the odds!

The strategy is less effective in four, six and eight-deck games where the overall number of the cards is less susceptible to composition changes from just a few cards being removed. For multiple-deck players, the news is not all bad though, for the basic strategies that we have presented in this book will bring you very close to an even game against the casino. Should you ever decide to improve your game further by learning a counting strategy, the strategies we've presented here are essential information anyway.

The optimal basic strategies for all deck games that we've presented in this book are 100% correct and the absolute best available.

Those readers desiring to further their edge over the house in blackjack, and to increase their profit expectancy, must learn either a counting system or the advanced non-counter strategy. See the back of the book for information on how to obtain the highly effective, but simple to use, *Cardoza Base Count Strategy*, the full *Home Instruction Course*, or the *Cardoza 1, 2, 3 Multiple Deck Non-Counter*.

GETTING THE MOST OUT OF THE CARDOZA NON-COUNTER STRATEGY

For those players who will be playing in Nevada, or other areas where there is a choice of games, it will be to your advantage to play in a single-deck game rather than a multiple deck one for the following two reasons:

- The single-deck game is inherently more favorable.
- The Cardoza Non-Counter strategy is most effective in a single-deck game because the single-deck game is highly sensitive to composition changes.

If you only have access to playing in multiple-deck games, you have two choices if you want to have the advantage over a multiple-deck game. Choice number one is that you can purchase the simple-to-use *Cardoza 1, 2, 3 Multiple Deck Non-Counter*. This will give you an edge of about ½ to 1% depending upon the particular conditions of the game and your skills.

The *Cardoza 1, 2, 3 Multiple Deck Non-Counter* strategy was developed for players who are intimidated by counting cards and it actually gives non-counting players the mathematical edge over the casino in multiple-deck games. This strategy is the result of our own research.

The second choice is the *Cardoza Base Count Strategy*, or even better, the *Cardoza School of Blackjack Home Instruction Course*, which is designed for serious players who want to work just a little harder.

These card counting strategies give you an edge of from 1% to 3% over the casino and put you on a professional level of play. The advanced count strategies and the exciting new *Cardoza 1, 2, 3 Multiple Deck Non-Counter* can be ordered through the coupons in the back of the book.

However, before anything else, you *must* learn the optimal basic strategies in this book if you want to be a winner. We can't stress this enough. You bought this book to learn how to win. So let's win!

Learn the strategies.

UNDERSTANDING THE GAMBLE

One of the realities of any gambling proposition is that no matter how well you play a game, if chance is involved, there will be times when you will experience terrible runs of bad luck. There is no way to predict when these runs will begin, how long they will last or when they will stop.

It is important to understand that just because you have an advantage over the house, it does not mean you will win every time. Having a bad losing streak is not necessarily a reflection on your playing abilities. Even the best players take beatings on occasion. With a small advantage in blackjack, the skillful player will be vulnerable to dizzying streaks of luck, both good and bad.

However, if a skill factor is involved in the gambling proposition, as in blackjack, that factor will eventually make the skillful player a winner. In the short run, luck goes back and forth, but as more and more hands get played out, skill begins to take its due and that is why it's so important to follow our winning strategies to the letter.

The bettor that sticks by his guns when things go poorly will find tremendous rewards when things go his way, for, in the end, a player with the skills of winning will be way ahead of the game—a big winner!

MONEY MANAGEMENT

Winning at blackjack requires not only the playing of the correct strategies but also the intelligent use of one's monetary resources. Blackjack is a very streaky game, and you can expect big winning and big losing streaks.

To emerge a winner from these pendulous swings of fortune takes a certain degree of emotional control, for the temptation to ride a winning streak too hard in the hopes of a big killing or to bet wildly during a losing streak, trying for a quick comeback, are two of the most common factors that destroy gamblers. Inevitably, big winning sessions dissipate into small wins or even disastrous losses while moderately bad losing sessions can turn into a nightmare.

Read this section carefully, for the difference between ending up a winner or a loser is heavily influenced by your skills in managing your money intelligently.

Money management skills can be divided into the following three categories:

1. **Emotional Control**
2. **Bankrolling** (Total bankroll, table bankroll).
3. **When to Quit** (Maximize gains, minimize losses).

Before we look at these skills more closely, there is one extremely important point that must be thoroughly understood.

> *Never gamble with money you cannot afford to lose*
> *either financially or emotionally.*

The importance of the rule highlighted in the box cannot be overemphasized.

Betting with money you cannot afford to lose adversely affects decision making. Rather than playing your best game, your strategy gets restricted to the confines of your monetary or emotional situation. Betting with "scared money" is a guaranteed way to ensure yourself a losing career as a gambler.

EMOTIONAL CONTROL

It is important to recognize that behind every bet you make is your money and your emotions, and that the ups and downs of your moods and feelings affect the quality of your play. For blackjack to be a pleasurable and successful experience every time you gamble, you must be aware of your state of mind and obey its needs.

Sometimes you won't feel 100%, perhaps you're having a day where your confidence or alertness is low. Accept and recognize that condition. As a human being, you experience moods, and will not always feel at your best. You must learn to recognize when your physical or emotional condition is affected and refrain from playing.

Whenever you feel emotionally unprepared to risk money, again, you should refrain from playing. And if, for whatever reason, the game becomes a cause of anxiety and ceases to be a form of entertainment, than it is time to take a breather. You won't play as well because your mind will be preoccupied by the possibility of losing and perhaps more importantly, you will receive no emotional satisfaction from the game.

Play again later on, when you're more alert and confident, and you will have the necessary ingredient of a winner—emotional control. Remember, the casinos aren't going anywhere. There's lots of time to get your bets down.

Manage your money intelligently and you will keep it working with you, and not against you.

BANKROLLING

A. Total Bankroll

To be a successful blackjack player, your bankroll must be large enough to withstand the normal fluctuations common to blackjack. Undercapitalization and overbetting are great dangers to the serious gambler. The player that consistently overbets will have larger winning sessions when he wins, but when he loses, he'll lose big. If a losing streak becomes extended, that player could be wiped out.

Playing with a bankroll large enough to sustain short run swings of bad luck is the only way to insure that your skill will bear long term results.

The following bankroll requirements have been prepared to give you enough capital to survive any reasonable losing streak, and be able to bounce back on top.

In the following table, **flat betting** refers to betting the same amount every time. When ranging bets from 1-4, you'll need a larger bankroll, for more money is wagered.

TOTAL BANKROLL REQUIREMENTS		
Hours to Play	Bet Range	Bankroll Needed
10	Flat	50 units
20+	Flat	100 units
10	1-4	150 units
20+	1-4	200 units

If you plan on playing for an extended weekend's worth of play (20 hours or more) at $5-$20 a hand, you should bring $1,000 with you, while if you are only planning to play 10 hours at those stakes, $750 will give you a fairly safe margin. This does not mean that you will lose this money playing $5-$20. Using the Cardoza Non-Counter betting strategy, you will have an edge on the house in a single- or double-deck game, and your expectancy is to win money every time you go.

However, it's important to be aware that just because you have an edge over the casino doesn't mean you're going to win. Losing streaks do occur. At a bet range of $5-$20, a loss of $500 is a real possibility. If the thought of losing amounts comparable to this during a downswing scares you, you should not play $5-$20 a hand, for you're betting over your head. Your bankroll and emotional frame of mind must be able to cope with bad losing streaks because they are part of the game.

Again, if you bet within your financial and emotional means, you will never regret a single session at the tables.

If you have a definite amount of money to play with and want to figure out how much your unit size bet should be, simply take your gambling stake and divide it by the amount of units you need to have.

Thus, if you bring $500 with you, and plan to play for 10 hours ranging your bets from 1-4, divide $500 by 150 units (see Total Bankroll Recommendations chart) and you will wager about $3 a hand. Betting more than $3 as a unit with only

$150 as a bankroll would be overbetting and leaving yourself vulnerable to being wiped out by a normal bad run of luck..

B. Table Bankroll

How much money should you bring to the table?

My recommendation is that your bring 30 units to the table each time you play. If playing $5 units, bring $150; if $2 units, bring $60. $25 bettors should bring $750. $100 bettors should sit down with $3,000.

TABLE BANKROLL RECOMMENDATIONS Bet Range: 1-4 Units		
Unit Bet	**Minimum Stake**	**Maximum Stake**
$1	$20	$30
$2	$40	$60
$5	$100	$150
$10	$200	$300
$25	$500	$750
$50	$1,000	$1,500
$100	$2,000	$3,000

You can bring less of a bankroll if you want. If **flat betting**, that is, betting the same amount on every hand, 15 units will suffice. If your bet range is from 1-4, 20 units will do the trick. However, do not bring more money to the table than 30 units. That is enough to cover normal fluctuations, and you never want to lose more than that in any one sitting.

WHEN TO QUIT

What often separates the winners from the losers is—the winners, when winning, leave the table a winner, and when losing, restrict their losses to affordable amounts. Smart gamblers never allow themselves to get destroyed at the table from one bad session.

As a player, you have one big advantage that, if used properly, will insure you success as a gambler—you can quit playing whenever you want to. To come out ahead, you must minimize your losses when you lose and maximize your gains when you win. This way, your winning sessions will eclipse your losing sessions and you will come out an overall winner.

MINIMIZING LOSSES

Here are three simple guidelines that, if followed, will save you a lot of money.

1. **Limit your table losses to 20 units (30 at the most).**

   If betting $5 chips, never lose more than $100 in any one session; if $2 units, then $40; if $25 units, then $500. Do not dig in for more money, and you can never be a big loser. Take a break, try again later. You never want to get into a position where losing so much in one session totally demoralizes you.

2. **Never increase your bet range beyond your bankroll capabilities.**

   In other words, always bet within your means.

3. **Never increase your bet size to catch up and break even.**

   Raising your bets to try and quickly win back losses will not change the odds of the game, nor will it change your luck. What it will do is make your chances of taking a terrible beating frighteningly high. As we discussed earlier, do *not* get into a position where losing so much in one session destroys any reasonable chance of coming out even.

It is essential to understand the following simple concept: You can't win all the time.

Rest awhile; you'll get them later.

MAXIMIZING GAINS

Following are two tried and true steps to maximize your winning sessions at blackjack. Incorporate these into your game and you will never walk away from a wining session with a single regret. Now, wouldn't that be a nice change?

1. **Once winning, the most important thing is to walk away a winner.**

   There is no worse feeling than leaving the blackjack table a loser after having been up a lot of money. Once your wins at a table have exceeded 20 units, put aside 10 units of your winnings, and play the other 10 units. If a losing streak ensues and you lose those 10 units, you have protected yourself. You walk away with 10 units in winnings!

2. **Set no limit on your winning sessions.**

   If your hot streak continues, keep putting wins aside into your "don't touch" pile. When your luck changes and you have lost the 10 unit buffer you have set aside to protect your guaranteed winning pile, you can quit a big winner.

SHOULD YOU INCREASE YOUR BET SIZE WHEN WINNING?

If you would like to try for a bigger win, the answer is yes, go for it—but in moderation. Do not get overzealous to the point that your hard-earned win is vulnerable to a few big losses. Increase your bets gradually when winning, keeping in mind that the more you bet, the more you risk losing.

One more thing to keep in mind. Just because you may have won six hands in a row doesn't mean that you'll win your seventh bet. You can just as easily lose that seventh hand as you could win it.

The theory on betting more at "hot" tables sounds good, but nobody has ever made a living following that strategy. In fact, many have gone bankrupt chasing that tooth fairy.

Mathematically, and in practice, only the odds of the game determines your chances of winning a particular play, not the won or lost results from a previous hand.

A WINNING REMINDER

If you learn your basic strategies perfectly, apply the Cardoza Non-Counter betting strategy, and follow the advice offered in this money management section, you will have the knowledge and skills to be a consistent winner at the 21 tables.

Having the advantage over the casino doesn't mean you will always win, as we discussed, but if you follow our advice to the letter, you should win a majority of the times you play, and overall be ahead of the game.

Good skill!

FAQ

(FREQUENTLY ASKED QUESTIONS)

I've received thousands of queries over the years regarding do's and don'ts in blackjack, the best plays to make, strange situations that occur, questions regarding odds and strategies, and of course, about my background and personal experiences at the game. Below, I'm including a sampling of the more popular and interesting questions, and hopefully, questions you would want to ask about the game of blackjack will be answered here.

Be sure to visit our website, **www.cardozabooks.com;** to find out more about our FREE gambling magazine with lots more questions and articles on blackjack and all the games. You can also see the catalog of books we publish here.

Let's now get to the questions.

BASIC STRATEGY

QUESTION

I keep hearing about Basic Strategy, but what exactly is that?

ANSWER

When players and authors refer to the "Basic Strategy," we're talking about the correct strategy to pursue knowing only three cards, your two hole cards and the dealer's upcard. This book shows you the correct basic strategy for the game of blackjack wherever it is played.

WHERE TO SIT

QUESTION

What is the best place to sit at the blackjack table? I have heard that the last player to receive the cards, the one at the dealer's right is in the most profitable position.

ANSWER

The seat you're referring to is called "third base," as opposed to "first base," the seat to the dealer's left which receives cards first. The third basemen gets to see all the cards played by the other players before he makes his strategy decision. Some players feel that the third baseman "controls" what card the dealer will draw since, in marginal hit and stand situations, he can draw and take away the card the dealer would have received, or he can stand and force the dealer to take a card he would not have otherwise been dealt. This belief of giving or taking away the dealer's card is a huge fallacy in blackjack, and we'll cover a bit more about this under Q and As coming up.

While the third base position is often better for card counters in a single-deck game, in a multiple-deck game, that advantage becomes insignificant. However, for the Basic Strategy player, all positions are equal; no one spot has any edge over any other one.

SPLITTING TENS

QUESTION

Am I allowed to split tens and is it a good play?

ANSWER

Not only can you split tens, but you can split any two ten-valued cards! For example, you can split a jack and a queen, a ten and a king, or any other "pair" of ten-valued cards. However, while the rules permit these plays, they are never good moves for the basic strategy player.

IS IT DIFFICULT TO COUNT CARDS?

QUESTION

I have heard it is really hard to count cards, that a player must be a genius. Is that so?

ANSWER

That's going too far. Card counters aren't necessarily even smart people, though they certainly are smart players. Card counting is fairly simple, so simple in fact that just about anyone can learn how to count cards in under one hour. It's that simple.

It is a mistaken notion that card counters memorize every card in the deck as it is played. Card counting is actually a system of keeping track of one set of cards against another. All a player needs to do to "count cards" is to memorize just one number in his or her head. Counters do not memorize every card played as most players think, in fact, very few people on earth could actually do that. You would really need a great memory to manage that feat.

There are different levels of card counting, but the basic skills needed to gain an edge over the casino—which anyone can do—can be learned and put to use after one practice session. It's that basic. The Cardoza School of Blackjack Home Instruction Course takes players through different skill levels, with the first level immediately providing the player with a mathematical advantage over the casino. More advanced levels increase that edge by giving the player more skills, but in reality, a player that wanted an edge without working too hard at the game would have a mathematical winning edge with just the first level.

The simplicity of counting cards really comes as a shock to just about everyone I have taught. My students can never get over it when I have them counting cards within one hour, and playing casino blackjack with an advantage the very next.

BLACKJACK: IS IT REALLY BEATABLE?

QUESTION

If the casino can be beaten at blackjack why do they offer the game? After all, they're not in business to lose money.

ANSWER

So few players follow the correct winning strategies at blackjack, if they even know them at all, that the game prospers and brings huge profits to the casinos. It has never failed to amaze me as to how few knowledgeable players there really are. After all, if every player out there followed my strategies, the casinos would shut down the game as we know it in two minutes.

But the fact remains that blackjack players as a group do not play correctly, preferring their home-grown strategies, beliefs, superstitions, and the like. As a result, casinos continue to make loads of money on the game. Yes, there are people that can beat the game, but when casinos identify these players, they bar them from play. Why more players don't learn the simple winning skills and take their game to a profitable level is always surprising to me.

SOFT AND HARD TOTALS

QUESTION

What are soft totals and hard totals?

ANSWER

Soft totals are hands which contain an ace that is used as 11 points, for example A3, a soft 14. Hard totals are hands where there is no ace or the ace counts as just one point. If the soft total of A3 drew a 10, the hand would now be a hard 14, or simply, a 14.

DOES THE THIRD BASEMEN INFLUENCE PLAY?

QUESTION

It seems that the third baseman has a big influence on what the dealer will draw. Your comments?

ANSWER

This is a fallacy. Sure, if the third basemen draws a card, the dealer will not get that card but the next one off the top of the deck. However, the card or cards this player chooses to take, or not take, could just as easily help one side as the other. Unless the third basement has knowledge of those upcoming cards, there is no validity that a good-playing third baseman will help or hurt your chances. It's the complete luck of the draw in this situation. That player's decision will help just as often as it will hurt.

AVERY'S BLACKJACK BACKGROUND

QUESTION

What age did you start gambling and how were you able to be successful?

ANSWER

I became a professional casino player before I was 21, and used disguises to make myself appear older. One of my favorite places to play was the old Dunes on the Las Vegas Strip, which has since been imploded and replaced by the Bellagio. I also liked playing at the Golden Gate, a grind joint in downtown Vegas which couldn't seem to beat me. (Incidentally, the Golden Gate used to make the best 99¢ shrimp cocktail in Vegas—now they're $1.99.) But of course, I spread my action everywhere in town, giving each casino a bang for my buck.

My success is predominately due to two factors. First, I learned the correct strategies studiously, and never deviated from the proper play whether I was winning or losing. The proper play was the proper play, and the proper bet was the proper bet, regardless of whether I won or lost the previous hand or had a bunch of bad sessions in a row.

The second factor, which I cannot emphasize enough if you plan on being a successful player, is being in control of your emotions and always exercising smart money management decisions. There were other skillful players I ran across, but the difference between me and them was that I always controlled the game, the game never controlled me. I wanted to beat the casino and win money, period. I was either up to my game and played it right, or I wasn't and I walked from the tables until I was ready to return with confidence and an edge.

I don't know how many otherwise skillful players I know or hear about that got buried in one disastrous losing session because their emotions ran away with them. They had the playing skills, but not the *emotional* ones.

CHANGING COLOR

QUESTION

What is the term used when players change in their chips for chips of different denominations.

ANSWER

It's called "coloring the money" or "changing color."

THE IDIOT ON THIRD

QUESTION

I remember playing on the Strip when the idiot playing third base at my table drew his 16 against the dealer's upcard of 6. He busted with, and I remember this card, the ten of clubs, the same ten of clubs that would have busted the dealer! Instead, the dealer flipped over a jack and then drew a 5 for a

21! I had $150 on a pat 20, my biggest bet of the night, and lost the hand. I could have killed him. I hate playing at tables where the third baseman makes bad plays and kills everyone's hands.

Anyway, I have two questions.

a. How much percentage do I lose when playing a table where the third baseman is an idiot like the guy who played at my table?

b. Do you recommend that I always watch the third baseman before I sit down to play?

ANSWER

Let's take each question, one at a time. To address your first concern. Many players find it annoying when the third basement "ruins" the hand for everyone else by making stupid plays. But the fact is, he'll ruin just as many hands for you with poor plays as he will help with other poor plays. You only remember those times when that draw didn't benefit you, not the times that you won because of his play. The dealer can just as easily draw a card that saves your hand as draw one that gives him a 20 or 21. It all averages out in the end. After all, how would you or he know that the next card will help or hurt you?

My own pet peeve is the double down situation of 11 against the dealer's 10. When I play, it seems that I receive more aces when doubling my 11 against the dealer's ace than all other cards put together. I don't know how many of you remember that dreaded ace on your own 11-point doubles. But if I calmly and rationally tracked all those instances, I would find that I received aces in the same proportion as other cards. That ace stands out in my mind, but it's an incidence of selective memory, not a real representation of what actually occurred.

As to your second question, while I think it is silly to "qualify" another player before you sit down at a table, if the play of the third baseman, or any other player for that matter, bothers you, simply leave the table, and go elsewhere where you can concentrate and have a better time. Never play at a table where something doesn't feel right or you're not enjoying yourself.

THE DOUBLING RULE

QUESTION

I'm confused about the doubling rule. When am I allowed to double down?

ANSWER

Doubling down is only allowed on the first two cards dealt to a player's hand, unless the rules allow doubling after splitting, in which case you may double down only on the first two cards of each split hand. You cannot double on the third card dealt to your original hand. For example, if you have a 3-2 and get dealt a 6, giving you 11 points, you may not double down—you can only hit.

INSURANCE

QUESTION

You should never go for insurance, is that right?

ANSWER

For beginning players, that is correct. Insurance is a bad bet and shouldn't be taken. Taking insurance blindly as a Basic Strategy player will be costly in the long run. Only card counters with knowledge of ten richness in a deck should take insurance.

INSURING BLACKJACKS

QUESTION

I've been told that you should always insure your blackjack. Is that a good strategy?

ANSWER

This is the same answer as in the previous question. Taking insurance is not good strategy. Keep in mind that insurance is a separate bet that the dealer has a ten-valued card under his hole card. Regardless of what hand you hold, be it a 20, a 16, or even when you hold your own blackjack, taking insurance is still a bad bet. In a single-deck game, insuring your blackjack against a dealer's ace is even a worse bet than normal since your blackjack removes one ten (out of sixteen total tens) that you're betting on the dealer to have. That's an 8% hit, which is a pretty heavy cut to give up on a bet.

SINGLE DECK OR MULTIPLE DECK

QUESTION

What is the best table to sit at: one, two, four, six, or eight decks? I've heard that single deck is the best. Is that true?

ANSWER

Yes it's true. Single-deck blackjack gives the player the best odds at blackjack. You have a dead-even game against the casino when playing single-deck Las Vegas Strip rules. The problem is that single-deck games are not as frequently seen as in the old days and often, in various locations, you have no choice but to play multiple-deck blackjack, because that may be all that is offered. That's okay though. While multiple-deck games are not as good as single-deck blackjack, they're still beatable, even by regular non-counters.

CAN YOU *REALLY* BEAT THE CASINO (REDUX)?

QUESTION

Can a player really have an advantage at blackjack and beat the casino?

ANSWER

Absolutely. The advantage is small, and depending on conditions, can be ½% to 2% or more. This book will put you at about an even game with the casinos, and with good rules in a single-deck game, at an advantage of ½% or more without even counting cards. Non-counters can also beat the multiple-deck game using the *Multiple Deck 1, 2, 3 Non-Counter Strategy*.

Casinos didn't bar me from playing blackjack for no reason. They knew I could beat them, and didn't want my action.

SHUFFLING: THE REAL REASON

QUESTION

Why do dealers shuffle before all the cards are used?

ANSWER

The casinos shuffle early purely as a protection against card counters. Before card counting became widespread and pit bosses began to take serious notice, casinos used to serve up predominately single-deck games and deal right down to the bottom of the deck. We're going back to the early 1980s on this one.

However, to protect the casinos from the new breed of card counter, casinos introduced multiple-deck games, and moved shuffle points up as a countermeasure against the card counters. These measures don't stop card counters entirely, and card counting is still effective, but early shuffling does reduce a counter's advantage. At the same time, extra shuffling reduces a casino's profit because they spend more time shuffling and less time dealing to average players, players who are going to give back much more money to the casino that the lone counter is earning.

IS AVERY CARDOZA ALLOWED TO PLAY?

QUESTION

Are you allowed to play blackjack in the casinos, and if not, is it legal to not allow particular players to gamble?

ANSWER

Disallowing a player to make wagers in a casino is called "barring" a player. I've been barred in many casinos. At one time, when I was playing professionally, my picture circulated throughout the Las Vegas casinos and I was being barred from clubs I hadn't even played in before! That's when I realized my playing days in Las Vegas were numbered. The difficulty in finding venues that would deal cards to me was the impetus that led to my very first book on gambling in 1981, the first edition of the book you're now holding in your hands, *Winning Casino Blackjack for the Non-Counter*.

As to the legalities of barring players, it has been challenged in court and upheld. Casinos are considered private clubs and may disallow any patron from their games. And believe me, they use that privilege. Whether it is right or not is another story, but with all the money that is generated by gaming revenue, and the way things work in gaming cities, it is not too presumptuous to think that other influences are at work when it comes to laws and gambling.

DEALERS WHO ARE TOO FAST

QUESTION

Dealers go too fast for me sometimes. What can I do about it?

ANSWER

One solution is to ask the dealer to slow down. Dealers will often try to rush players, but hey, you're the patron. If a dealer goes too fast for you and doesn't respond to your request to slow down, simply slow down your own play. They can't go past your spot until you make your stand or hit decision anyway. If the dealer continues to be annoying, switch tables. Play where you are comfortable and can enjoy the game.

MY ACQUAINTANCE ALWAYS WINS: HOW?

QUESTION

An acquaintance of mine wins every time he plays. I don't know what his secret strategy is because he won't tell me. So let me ask you. How does he do it?

ANSWER

For starters, he *says* he wins every time he plays. That's a lot different than actually winning. One method of winning every time is by being delusional. Another method is to be a large casino dealing out hands to hundreds of players and having an edge on just about every one of them, if not all of them.

The reality of this player, though, is that he is most likely a compulsive loser who, between his wins, conveniently forgets about his losses. Nobody wins every time, not myself or any other professional. Don't think for one second that anything resembling reality is emitting from the lips of players who say they win all the time. Believe me, I hear from these type of gamblers all the time, many of whom can't scrape two nickels together to make friction. I would love to play the house and deal to this type of gambler all night and day.

I have spent many hours at the tables as a professional, and while I am able to win a majority of times, I can't do it every time.

GETTING THE ROYAL TREATMENT

QUESTION

My friend's father is a great gambler. Casinos fly him in first class, with room, board, shows, the works. And he comes home every time with thousands of dollars in profits. He seems to live the great life courtesy of the casinos. How can I get the royal treatment like him?

ANSWER

Easy. Lose as much money as he does and they would be treating you just as good. If he dropped that much money in my casino, I would also fly him in first class. I have no doubt that your friend's father lives the great life courtesy of the casinos. Executives of the major casinos know how to treat their high rollers real good. But he is paying through the nose for these privileges. The casinos have lavish suites for their high rollers, called "whales," and these whales drop loads of cash when they visit.

When a player is getting flown in and treated first class, the casino is making up for its expenditures in a big way. (Note: there are some card counters who do get first-class treatment and win money at the same time—I'm just discussing the general run of gamblers.) These first-class trips are not free vacations, not the way I see it. These players *are* getting the royal treatment—but not the royal treatment they think they're getting!

IS CARD COUNTING CHEATING

QUESTION

I've heard that casinos not only don't like card counting, but consider is cheating. Is it?

ANSWER

Not by any stretch of the imagination. The casinos would like to make that case, but it is a shallow and devious argument. Bottom line, you are playing by their rules. There is nothing wrong with using your skills to beat a game that contains skillful elements. And there is certainly elation when you successfully do that.

DOES AVERY CARDOZA ALWAYS WIN AT 21?

QUESTION

I love your books and see that you really know the game, but curiosity has the best of me on this one: Do you win every time you play?

ANSWER

I get asked this question often, so I've included this additional Q and A on the subject because it gives me another opportunity to talk about the realities and expectations of blackjack, and more importantly, money management.

To answer the question: I win most of the time, but not all the time. There would be nothing unusual about me, or any other professional, losing three sessions in a row. Ups and downs are normal in blackjack and any other form of gambling. Losing streaks cannot be helped. What can be helped is how you respond to bad luck—minimizing its ill effects or falling prey to it and getting hammered beyond repair.

I don't win every time because I cannot control the cards I receive, only what I do with them. If I am dealt lousy cards all night, I'm going to lose, and there is nothing I can do about it. And if I'm dealt good cards all night, I will win. What separates me from the average player is that I always play correctly regardless of my daily results, and when all the bad and good sessions are mixed together, the edge I have over the casino will prevail, and I will win money playing blackjack.

There is only one correct way to play, and the winner never deviates from that way just because he or she is mired in a losing streak. Losing is part of the game. You can't win every hand you're dealt, or every session you play in. But you can win money by sticking to your guns and playing the correct way all the time.

WHEN IS TIME TO QUIT?

QUESTION

When should I leave a table?

ANSWER

For Basic Strategy players, the simple answer is that you should walk away from a table whenever you have reached your loss limit for the session (see the "Money Management" chapter). You must always have a reasonable loss limit that makes sense. You should also take a break when emotionally you're just not up for the game, for whatever reason—fatigue, distractions, feeling unlucky—whatever.

ARE LIVE LESSONS STILL AVAILABLE?

QUESTION

Do you still teach players how to beat blackjack?

ANSWER

I rarely teach players in person anymore, my time has become too scarce with all the projects I work on. That is why I have written the winning strategies we sell, the Cardoza Base Count Strategy, the Cardoza School of Blackjack Home Instruction Course, and the 1, 2, 3 Multiple Deck Non-Counter, with the same care and step-by-step thinking as in this book.

IS IT POSSIBLE TO WIN WITHOUT COUNTING?

QUESTION

Can I beat the casino without counting cards?

ANSWER

Absolutely. This book shows you how to bring the house advantage down to nothing by using the Basic Strategy and, in single- and double-deck games, to use our non-counter strategy to actually take the edge. The multiple-deck game can be beat without counting cards, but only by using the Multiple Deck 1, 2, 3 Non-Counter Strategy.

BURNING CARDS AND STRATEGY

QUESTION

The casinos always burn cards after they shuffle, and before they begin dealing. Some even burn cards after every deal. How does that affect my strategy?

ANSWER

For those unfamiliar with the term, *burning* is when a card is removed from play without actually having been put into play. Whether a casino burns one card, or many, these unplayed cards have no bearing on your chances of winning and do not affect play. A burned card may as well be the last few cards in the deck for all you care; in either case, they won't be played and you won't know what they are.

PLAYING WITH A FULL TABLE OR SOLO

QUESTION

Do I have a better chance of winning with a full table of players, or just with myself alone or perhaps one other player?

ANSWER

While the number of players at a table do not affect your chances of winning one way or the other, they do change the speed of play. The more players at a table, the slower the game goes, particularly in a single-deck game where, at a table of five or more players, only two rounds can be played before the cards are shuffled.

The game will also go slower because the dealer must spend more time dealing and collecting cards, taking and paying bets, and awaiting the decision of every additional player at a table.

BECOMING A PROFESSIONAL PLAYER

QUESTION

How does a person become a professional player? I've always loved the idea of beating the casino and making my living at it. What advice do you have?

ANSWER

Playing professionally means earning your living at blackjack. I don't encourage readers to drop their day jobs to pursue this profession because it is a tough living. You not only have to deal with the fact that casinos don't want your type of player there, but also, you must be able to handle the stress of losing streaks, which *will* occur. Not many players can handle that kind of stress and stick firmly to the strategies required to win.

To play blackjack professionally, you must have enough of a bankroll to handle the up and down streaks that are so inherent in this game, have the emotional capacity to deal with the angry looks and "heat" the casino will heap on you, plus you must be able to weather the losing streaks that are a part of this game. You also have to be well versed in a solid professional level card counting strategy. Above all, you must have the confidence and mental fortitude to play perfectly at all times regardless of the conditions or your emotional frame of mind. That's a lot to ask of a player and is the reason why there are so few blackjack pros out there.

In any case, before you can even consider playing professionally, you must be able to prove that you can win consistently at the tables. It's one thing to win at home or be up after ten hours of casino play, it's another thing to do this day in and day out as a professional. My advice: Find an easier line of work.

However, if you are devoted to blackjack, by all means, give it your best as a casual or serious player. Learn a professional strategy to increase your odds and take their money home with you.

That's the plan that makes the most sense of all.

IMPROVING
YOUR SKILLS

INTRODUCTION

In this chapter, I have put together a simple five-step plan to get you ready for practicing blackjack, to be followed by the next chapter, which gives you three quizzes to hone your skills further. Every ½% you gain means more money in your pocket and less in the casino's. I like that scenario a whole lot better than going to the tables unprepared and being at a disadvantage.

First though, let's have a small discussion on the effects of being unprepared, or to put it in another way, being the "average" player who plays without any real concern to winning.

EXPECTED RESULTS

Blackjack is a game where every decision you make affects your percentage expectation against the house. If you play poorly, you can give up more than 3%, or even 5% overall to the casino. That may not sound like much, but when you multiply, say 3%, by every single bet you make—which is how the math works out—that adds up to a lot of money quickly.

For example, if you bet an average of $10 per play, and kick back for three hours at a blackjack table, that's a total of $2,400 in action assuming eighty hands per hour ($10 per hand x 80 hands is $800 in action per hour). A 3% house edge will give you an expected loss of $72 over that stretch. At ten hours of play, you're looking at a $240 loss. If instead, you averaged $20 per hand, that loss would be $480. Your expected loss would be even higher if you bet more per hand, played more hands per hour, or played more hours.

Those losses at a 3% disadvantage will add up quickly, in fact, *six times* as quickly as a player going against just a ½% nut. You probably would like to pay less taxes on your income, why pay more to the casinos then?

Think about it.

The more action on the table, the more losses will be over the long run. For example, if you're a quarter ($25 chip) or dollar ($100 chip) player, those expected losses will be much greater, of course, than the examples above. If you didn't know what you were doing and were experiencing big losses at the table, now you have a better understanding of what went wrong.

The numbers I show above, of course, are expected results over the long run. In the short term, results will not go according to percentages and will vary wildly, as we all know. Sometimes you'll win, sometimes you'll lose, regardless of your skill level. That's the nature of gambling. However, like water seeking it's lowest level, percentages will play themselves out as well, and over time, will take their rightful toll.

TURNING THE TABLES

But let's look at the other side of the coin. What if, instead, you were better prepared and played at only a ½% disadvantage at an average of $10 per hand for twenty hours? Instead of losing $480, you would be out an average of only $80. That's a $400 difference for a relatively short amount of time.

Multiply these numbers by many sessions and many trips and we're talking about a significant amount of money!

Now let's take that one step further and say you had that ½% edge. Now *you* have that winning expectation of $80, not the house.

Do you see what am I getting at?

The picture begins to look better every time we up your skill level. When you are prepared to play blackjack for money and truly want to win, you can expect different results. Why not give your gambling money the same careful consideration as your other money concerns in life? Or to look at it another way, why not give yourself the enjoyment of knowing you're playing a tough game against the casino, perhaps with an advantage. It's always a blast to beat the casinos, certainly a lot more fun and more profitable than losing.

It's one thing to think you know what the proper strategy decisions are, it's another to actually make those correct decisions when you are under the bright lights.

Let's look at some ways to get ready for live play. I'm assuming you read this book carefully, understand the rules of the game and your playing options, and have studiously and carefully read my advice on money management.

Okay, let's get started.

FIVE STEPS TO BECOMING A WINNING BLACKJACK PLAYER

Step One

Reread the strategy section and study the basic strategy charts. Get comfortable not only with the correct plays you should make, but the logic behind those plays. This will make learning the strategies easier and keep you focused on why certain plays should be made all the time, regardless of whether you're losing or winning.

Step Two

Give yourself self-tests on various strategy situations to see if you have remembered the correct plays. You do this until you have the strategy down cold.

Step Three

Deal out practice hands to yourself, giving the dealer his upcard as well. Get comfortable making plays with this simulated situation. Every time you are uncertain of the correct play, look it up in the strategy charts. You should deal out hands over and over again until you can make the correct decision on every situation that comes up.

Step Four

Have someone deal out hands to you so that you get the feel of playing against a dealer. This is as close to a simulation as you can get without being in the casino. This will let you practice with a dealer controlling the pace, not you. If you can play flawlessly without referencing the strategy charts, you're ready to play casino blackjack with all your guns going.

Step Five

You've practiced by yourself, you've studied the charts, and you've also practiced with a simulated dealer. There is one more step to get you to maximum efficiency as a Basic Strategy player: Score 100% on the quizzes in the following chapter. If you do well here, you're a tough Basic Strategy player, and that will make you better than 95% of the other blackjack players at the tables. If you ace these, you're ready for live action.

PRACTICE STRATEGY QUIZZES

This chapter is designed to help get you prepared to play blackjack for real money in casinos. As I've stressed throughout this book, playing perfect Basic Strategy is essential to your goal of beating the dealer. You want to get every edge you can and, at the same time, remove any advantage the casino might have. Winning blackjack all starts with knowing how to play every hand correctly. You want to know what to do in every situation on paper so when you're playing live, you have no trouble making the right moves and giving yourself every chance to beat the casino at blackjack. That's the point of testing your knowledge against these quizzes.

The quizzes are divided into three sections, with 12 questions each. The first section contains the Basic Plays, the second contains the Intermediate Plays, and the third, the Tough Basic Strategy Plays. These questions assume knowledge of only three cards, the dealer's upcard and the two in your possession. We are also assuming Las Vegas Strip rules, no doubling after splitting, and no surrender allowed.

Answers with detailed explanations follow. Knock 'em out, partner.

In the following quizzes, the 10 is used interchangeably with the jack, queen and king since they are all 10-valued cards. So when I use the symbol "10," it could mean any of the picture cards or the 10 itself.

PRACTICE STRATEGY QUIZZES

BASIC PLAYS

1	K♣	2♠	VS.	6♦
2	5♠	5♣	VS.	10♦
3	8♣	9♦	VS.	8♠
4	10♠	K♣	VS.	9♥
5	J♣	Q♥	VS.	6♥
6	3♣	2♣	VS.	7♥
7	8♥	8♣	VS.	6♣
8	6♠	5♦	VS.	8♣
9	3♥	3♣	VS.	K♠
10	4♣	5♥	VS.	8♥
11	A♠	A♦	VS.	A♥
12	K♦	6♠	VS.	Q♣

DETAILED ANSWERS TO BASIC PLAYS

1. 10 2 VERSUS 6

Stand in this situation. Never bust a 12 when the dealer holds this stiff card. The dealer will bust 42% of the time on average when showing a 6 as the upcard. You'll lose in the long run with this hand, but you'll lose a lot less by standing rather than hitting. Remember, once you bust, you lose regardless of whether the dealer busts as well after.

2. 55 VERSUS 10

Take a hit. Splitting is not an option here, not against the powerful 10, and not with two fives. With 55 in fact, you'll never split under any conditions. Doubling down on 10 versus 10 is also not an option. The correct play is the most mundane, simply draw until you get 17 or higher. Thus, if your next card is a 3, you'll need to draw again since now you'll only have 13.

3. 89 VERSUS 8

Stand in this situation. Always stand on hard 17 against any dealer upcard. There are too many draws that will bust you. You're an underdog here, but that's much better than busting and having no chance at all.

4. 10 10 VERSUS 9

Stand. You're in like Flint with a 20. Hold your horses. You're a huge favorite. If you got dealt 20s all day long, you would make more money, more quickly than you can imagine. Too bad that's not the reality. The point though, is that 20 is a great hand. Don't even consider splitting this hand, especially against a dealer pat card.

5. 10 10 VERSUS 6

Stand. The Basic Strategy player should never split tens. You're very strong, the dealer is very weak. The basic strategy rule in blackjack is to stay with winners and take the bird in the hand. Only a card counter would make an exception to this rule, but that would be under very unusual circumstances. Their usual play as well would be to stand. Splitting tens will cost you about 15% in the long run. That's a big loss.

6. 32 VERSUS 7

This is an obvious draw. Never stand with any total hard 11 or less. That would be insane. You can only make the hand stronger. No possible draw will either weaken your total or bust you. Anyone that stands in this situation needs their head examined. With a measly 5 total, doubling is never an option either, no matter what the dealer shows.

7. 88 VERSUS 6

Split. The total of 16 is the worst hand you can have. But since this 16 is comprised of a pair of 8s, you have the opportunity to make two decent hands out of one lousy one. This is a huge gain.

8. 65 VERSUS 8

Double down. It's always correct to double down with an 11 in a single-deck game, no matter what card the dealer holds. (In a multiple-deck game, you would double down against all cards but the dealer's ace.) You have a big advantage here with a hand that will make you a lot of money in the long run.

9. 33 VERSUS 10

This is a clear draw. You would never split 3s against such a powerful dealer upcard. You have a bad hand, no sense making it two bad hands. Of course, with only a 6 total, standing wouldn't be a smart option either.

10. 45 VERSUS 8

Take a hit. You have a good hand, and will have a great relative hand if a 10 is drawn. While you are in a strong position, doubling is never an option with a 9 against a dealer's

8. Doubling against this upcard would only be wise with the powerful player totals of 10 or 11.

11. AA VERSUS A

Split. It is always correct to split aces, whether it's single deck, multiple deck or the dealer shows an ace, as in this example (or a 10, 2 or any other upcard for that matter).

12. 10 6 VERSUS 10

Draw. This is a close play, but the correct move for Basic Strategy players is to draw. Overall, this is the worst hand you can have and you will lose roughly 75% of the time. However, there is a gain by drawing. Card counters will often deviate and stand in this situation due to their increased knowledge of ten richness or poorness, but it would be an incorrect move for the average player who didn't possess the game information known by a card counter.

PRACTICE STRATEGY QUIZZES

	INTERMEDIATE PLAYS			
1	8♠ 8♦		VS. 3♥	
2	8♣ 8♥		VS. 10♦	
3	9♥ 2♦		VS. J♠	
4	7♠ 7♣		VS. 3♥	
5	2♦ 2♣		VS. 2♥	
6	Q♥ 6♣		VS. A♥	
7	A♦ 2♣		VS. K♥	
8	7♠ 7♣		VS. 8♣	
9	Q♥ 3♣		VS. 2♦	
10	9♥ 9♦		VS. J♠	
11	A♠ 6♣		VS. 7♥	
12	A♣ 8♥		VS. 4♣	

135

DETAILED ANSWERS TO INTERMEDIATE PLAYS

1. 88 VERSUS 3

Split. Eights are always split. In this instance, there is a big gain as a poor starting total of 16 is made into two reasonably strong totals of 8 each against the dealer's stiff 3.

2. 88 VERSUS 10

Split. Again, eights are always split. While this is a poor hand to hold, computer studies show that two starting totals of 8 each are superior to holding the worst starting hand of all, the 16. Overall, you will lose money with this hand, but less money than if the hand was drawn to.

3. 92 VERSUS 10

Double down. The 11 is the most powerful doubling down total and leads to huge overall gains for a player. The 10 is a tough dealer upcard, but our 11 is a more powerful hand.

4. 77 VERSUS 3

Split. Sevens are correctly split against the dealer's 3s through 7s in single and multiple-deck games, and additionally, 2s in the single-deck game. Two starting totals of 7 each is far superior to one starting total of 14.

5. 22 VERSUS 2

Draw. It is never correct to split a pair of 2s against the dangerous dealer 2 (unless the game allows doubling after splitting, when it would be the correct play). The dealer has too many ways to make a hand. He will make an 18 or better hand 51% of the time, and with our starting totals of 2, that is too much fire to fight with extra money at risk.

6. 10 6 VERSUS A

Draw. The dealer busts only 17% of the time starting with an ace. You've got to make a better hand to have a chance here. Standing would be a terrible play.

7. A2 VERSUS 10

Draw. This is a fairly straightforward play. You wouldn't consider doubling against the 10 with a hard or soft 13, nor would you stand with a soft total here.

8. 77 VERSUS 8

Draw. We are in a disadvantageous situation, and while we will take advantage against weaker dealer upcards to split, against a potential dealer 18, we don't want more money out on two potential 17s. It's best here just to take our knocks with the starting total of 14 and hope for the best with our draw.

9. 10 3 VERSUS 2

Stand. With a starting total of 13, you never want to risk going over 21 against a dealer bust card. Don't confuse this hand with the player 12 versus dealer 3 situation, where we actually take a hit. Our big disadvantage in going first is once we bust, we lose, even if the dealer bust afterwards. That busting-first factor is the difference between a player's hand of 13 compared to a player's hand of 12.

10. 99 VERSUS 10

Stand. While we can gravitate to a stronger total of 19 each with a split, this is not the time nor is it a good move against the very powerful dealer upcard of 10. Our 18 as it stands is not great, only a fair total in this situation, but it sure beats doubling our money into an inferior situation.

11. A6 VERSUS 7

Draw. No matter the situation, you should never stand with a soft 17. You'll double down against all dealer bust cards (except against the 2 in a multiple-deck game, where you'll simply draw), but otherwise, it is a very large gain to draw to the soft 17. Only weak players stand with this terrible starting total of 17. Hard 17s we will stand on, because the chances of busting are too high to consider drawing. But when you have a shot at improving, as we do here when the hand is soft, you've got to draw.

12. A8 VERSUS 4

Stand. A 19 is a very strong starting total, and though the hand is soft, it is a poor play to double down and risk the very solid possibilities of winning for all sorts of draws that will make this hand vulnerable to a loss. As we have discussed in this book, with a few exceptions, hands with very solid chances for winning should not be broken up to go after additional winnings by splits or doubles.

PRACTICE STRATEGY QUIZZES

TOUGH PLAYS

#	Player Hand		VS.	Dealer
1	A♥	7♣	VS.	K♣
2	10♦	2♥	VS.	2♠
3	9♦	2♥	VS.	A♠
4	A♥	7♦	VS.	2♣
5	9♠	9♥	VS.	8♠
6	9♦	9♣	VS.	7♥
7	9♣	9♠	VS.	A♣
8	6♠	3♥	VS.	2♦
9	A♥	2♣	VS.	6♠
10	A♦	6♣	VS.	5♥
11	4♠	4♥	VS.	3♣
12	7♠	7♥	VS.	7♣

DETAILED ANSWERS TO TOUGH PLAYS

1. A 7 VERSUS 10

Hit! Beginners don't make this play, but savvy players do. 18 is only a fair hand, and against the tough 10, we need to try and improve if possible. The soft total gives us the possibility. Obviously, with a hard 18, we would never draw, for almost any card would bust that draw, but nothing will bust this soft hand. You'll be surprised how often you land the 3 or 2 and it makes the hand. If you draw a poor card, say a 7 for a new total of hard 15, you'll need to draw again since correct strategy calls for hitting hard 15 against a 10.

2. 10 2 VERSUS 2

The correct play is to hit. This is one of the two exceptions to not drawing with bust hands against a dealer bust card (the other being when the dealer has a 3 against our 12). The combination of us having more ways to make a hand and the dealer busting less frequently with the dangerous 2 (as well as the less dangerous 3), makes hitting in this situation the correct play.

3. 92 VERSUS A

Hit in a multiple-deck game; double down in a single-deck game. The 11 is a very powerful player total and will always be doubled against all upcards by the Basic Strategy player except for multiple-deck games where the 11 doesn't have quite enough juice to make it profitable to double against the ace. But against the 10, doubling down is the correct play.

4. A7 VERSUS 2

Stand. This is a tough play to remember for many players, but a strong play, nevertheless. You're strong with the 18 against the 2, but not strong enough to double as you would against the slightly higher busting potential of the dealer 3. Yet, you do not want to risk weakening the 18 by drawing. Hanging tight and standing is the best way to go.

5. 99 VERSUS 8

Split. The 9s are tricky plays. Two potential winners is better than one potential draw any day. There is a big gain by splitting here.

6. 99 VERSUS 7

Stand! The dealer's total gravitates toward a 17, and your 18 in hand beats that. While splitting will also make you money in the long run, it won't make you as much as standing with your big potential winner.

7. 99 VERSUS A

Stand. These 9s can get confusing until you understand the logic behind the plays. An 18 is only fair, but with the very low busting potential of the dealer's ace (the dealer will only bust 17% of the time with an ace as an upcard), you cannot afford to put more money out by splitting this hand.

8. 63 VERSUS 2

Draw in a multiple-deck game; double down in a single-deck game. This is one of those close plays that is affected by the number of cards in the starting pack. A potential 19 is a strong starting total, but against the versatile dealer 2, there is not quite enough gain to be made in a multiple-deck game to justify doubling the money on this hand.

9. A2 VERSUS 6

Double down. The dealer has a weak upcard. Soft totals are unusual doubling hands because we're not actually looking to get a 10 as we would with the hard doubling totals but prefer "softer" cards, in this instance, in descending order of preference, the 8, 7, 6, 5, and 4. The 2, 3 and ace are also not too bad, as you'll have a redraw and still can't bust. Doubling with this soft total is a big gain because we're capitalizing on high dealer busting possibilities which gives us an automatic win no matter what we draw. At the same time, we have good chances of making strong hands ourself that can prove to be winners even if the dealer draws out a total of 17 or better.

10. A6 VERSUS 5

Double down. We go after the very weak dealer upcards, doubling our bet in situations where we will win more than we will lose. Of course, you will lose this hand sometimes, But blackjack must be seen as a game of percentages. In the long run, always making the correct plays will make you money. Don't worry about the short view and a few losses here and there with these plays. If you do that, you'll give the edge back to the casino, and that is what they're counting on. Always make the right play.

11. 44 VERSUS 3

Draw. You'll never split 4s in this situation, even in games that allow doubling after splitting. (In those games 4s are only split against the dealer's 5 and 6 upcards.) When doubling after splitting is not an option, 4s are never split against any dealer upcard. One reasonably starting total of 8 is way better than two bad starts of 4 each.

12. 77 VERSUS 7

Split. While the 7 is a weak dealer upcard, interestingly enough, it will form weaker average hands than the bust cards when a hand of 17 or better is made. It won't bust as often as the 2-6 upcards, but the large number of 10-value cards will gravitate this hand toward a 17. So we adjust as well, and take the weak 14 into two playable totals that gravitate toward 17 as well, keeping us in the ballgame. Splitting this hand is a gain.

FIFTEEN POINTS OF 21 ETIQUETTE

Like all games, blackjack has its own unique code of conduct. You won't look like a pro right out of the gate, but understanding the following fifteen rules of etiquette will make your blackjack experience as smooth as possible.

1. USE ONLY ONE HAND TO HOLD THE CARDS

The casinos want you to use only one hand when holding your two cards. The reason is simple: It's a precaution against players switching cards, which is harder to do one-handed. For the very same reason, players are supposed to handle the dice one-handed in craps games.

2. DON'T REMOVE YOUR CARDS FROM VIEW OR OFF THE TABLE

Taking your cards out of the view of the dealer is a big no-no in blackjack. Casinos are always on the alert for cheaters. Keeping your cards in plain sight at all times is one of the ways they keep the game honest. It's not that you're doing anything underhanded, but the house wants to make sure no one else is.

3. DON'T TOUCH YOUR CHIPS ONCE THE CARDS HAVE BEEN DEALT

Once the cards have been dealt, you are not supposed to touch your bet. This is another way the casinos try to maintain the integrity of the game—or at least their bankroll. They are always on the alert for players that top off their bets after they have received big hands or after the outcome is determined, called *past posting*.

4. DON'T TOUCH YOUR CARDS WHEN THEY ARE DEALT FACE UP

In games that are dealt from a shoe (as opposed to handheld single- and double-deck games), your cards will be dealt face up. Of course, it is not a disadvantage if the dealer can see your cards, because he is bound by strict standing and hitting rules. When the cards are dealt face up, you are not allowed to handle them as you would in games where your cards are dealt face down. In face-up games, signal your playing intentions by hand signals, which takes us to the next point.

5. INDICATE ALL PLAYING DECISIONS USING HAND SIGNALS

Regardless of the type of game you're playing, single or multiple deck, you should *always* indicate your playing intentions by physical actions. If you want to hit, point to the felt or scrape your cards. If you decide to stand, wave your hand crossways over your cards or bet, or push your cards under your chips. If you double or split, put more chips on the table to indicate an increased bet. In all these instances, your intentions will be clear. Verbal instructions can be misunderstood, which is why casinos insist on physical actions as the determination of your playing intention.

6. WHEN DOUBLING OR SPLITTING, DON'T STACK YOUR CHIPS ON TOP OF THE ORIGINAL PILE

The correct way to double your bet when you are doubling or splitting is to place your additional chips next to the original bet, not on top of it. The reason is simple: It is very easy for a player to increase his original bet by piling it on, obscuring the original bet and making a new, bigger bet to the casino's disadvantage. Casinos, of course, don't want to give players an unfair and illegal advantage. That is why they insist that you line up your chips next to the original stack.

7. BE SURE TO REMOVE WON CHIPS FROM YOUR BETTING AREA

After a winning hand, the dealer will place your winnings next to your original bet. If you become distracted—let's say you're ordering a drink, engaging in a conversation, or doing something else that distracts your attention—it is possible that the dealer will think you're letting your bet ride for the next hand. If that is your intention, fine. But if it isn't, you may inadvertently end up with a too-large bet and a too-large loss. Of course, you could get lucky and win. However, as a general rule, make sure to immediately service won bets so that you, and not fate, is in control of your betting amount. Note that betting more chips than you desired can more easily happen if the dealer colors your won bet, thus making only one pile in the betting area.

8. PAY ATTENTION TO THE AMOUNT YOU HAVE BET

Mistakes do happen. With the number of tasks the dealer is performing—shuffling, dealing, adding up totals, adding up won bet amounts, paying off splits, doubles and blackjacks—and the usual speed of doing these things, it is impossible for the dealer not to mess up here and there. It is up to you to protect your bets, making sure that when you win, you're paid off and that you're paid the right amount. If you think a mistake has been made, tell the dealer immediately while the chips are still in the betting area. Once the next hand is dealt, it is too late to rectify the problem.

9. COLOR UP WHEN YOU LEAVE THE TABLE

Dealers like to keep their small checks (chips) at the table so that they have enough chips to pay off other bettors. If you've accumulated many smaller chips and are ready to cash out, give the dealer an opportunity to "color them up," that is, exchange the smaller chips for ones of higher denominations. This is also helpful to you because you will be able to manage, say five $100 chips more easily than one hundred $5 chips.

10. PUT YOUR BIG CHIPS ON BOTTOM

When you make bets comprised of multiple denominations, the dealer will request that your higher denomination chips go on bottom, and the lower ones on the top. Actually, he will do that for you and request that you do it yourself next time. The reason for this policy is to protect against players manipulating the big chips. It is much easier to add or remove a chip from the top of the stack than from the bottom, so casinos protect themselves by making sure the small chips are on top.

11. DON'T ANNOY OTHER PLAYERS OR SLOW UP THE GAME

It's okay to chitchat, have fun and liven up a blackjack table—as long as it doesn't interfere with the enjoyment of other players or slow down the game. In other words, if you have a long story to tell, maybe the 21 table is not the right place to do it. Similarly, don't get involved in off-the-table conversations with bystanders, talk on your cell phone, or do anything else that interferes with the normal speed of the game. The other players at the table are there to play blackjack, not listen to you or watch your activities.

12. DO NOT CRITICIZE OTHER PLAYERS' DECISIONS

All players have the right to make the strategy moves they deem correct and to bet as much or as little as they desire. The other players are playing their own money, not yours. Just because a player may be hitting a hard 18, standing on 12 versus 6, or splitting 10s does not give you the right to criticize that player. Minding your own business is just common courtesy. If a player has paid for the privilege of receiving cards, he has the right to play them as he sees fit.

13. TIPPING IS CUSTOMARY

As in a restaurant, tipping for good service is expected. It is up to you to decide if you want to tip and how much. The customary tipping method is to make a bet for the dealer alongside one of your own bets. Simply place a bet alongside your own bet, indicating that it is for the dealer. This is the best way to tip because when you win, the dealer wins double—the tip amount that you bet plus the winnings from that bet. Naturally, the dealer will be rooting for you to win.

14. NEVER HAND MONEY OR CHIPS DIRECTLY TO THE DEALER

As a protection against cheating, physical contact with blackjack personnel is not allowed. When you want to color up or down, or get chips, place your chips or cash on the table and let the dealer pick up the currency from there.

15. DON'T BE A POOR SPORT

A certain amount of complaining is expected when the cards don't go your way, losses mount up, or a winning streak is stymied. But nobody at the blackjack table or anywhere else in life, wants to be around a moaner. Take your losses like a champ to keep the game as fun as it can be, despite the bad mojo.

TEN MORE QUESTIONS AND ANSWERS

Here are ten more questions—and a bonus one—I've received from readers over the years and the answers I've given them. You may have some of these questions yourself. My answers and the reasoning behind them should give you a better understanding of blackjack.

1. WHEN TO QUIT A SESSION

QUESTION

I was at a big Indian casino and had $1,000 in winnings from slots and roulette, and then decided to play in the high roller area at a $50 blackjack table. It was a slow time, so many tables were empty. They opened a table for me, and because it was slow, the pit boss and dealers were very friendly and I felt comfortable. I was soon joined by four players who came and then left during the hour I was there, leaving me alone again. I was pretty happy, though, being up $1,600 at the table, giving me a total of $2,600 in winnings in just a few short hours.

But after the other players left. I started losing the one-on-one game with the dealer and went down to $200 in winnings. I felt like a loser, even though I was still ahead, but I was almost embarrassed to stop as they had pampered me and I was the only one at the table. I hung on and lost that $200 and then $200 more. "Enough is enough!" I said to myself and finally walked away, slightly disgusted that I gave all the winnings back. Even the pit boss said, "You should have stopped when you were ahead."

Let's say that you have just sat down at a full table, but you feel like you've had enough, or like my experience above, you're really not feeling it anymore. I hate jumping tables because I like to get comfortable, but sometimes you just can't stay at one that looked as good as it did previously. How many hands should you play before you leave?

ANSWER

The answer is easy. Leave any time you are uncomfortable or ready to go, regardless of any other situation. It's your money—you have the option to play or not play, be it one hand, two hands, a hundred hands, or even no hands at all. Even if casino personnel go out of their way to accommodate you, move on when you are ready to go. You are the customer. They dance to your music. The casino and its pit bosses couldn't care less if you lose all your money; in fact, they would be happy if you did. If you're up a bunch of money, go have a great dinner, preferably on the house, and walk away knowing you're the winner. That's a great feeling, certainly much better than knowing you could have walked away a winner but didn't.

When you make the right decisions about quitting, you'll always come out ahead.

2. ONLINE BLACKJACK STRATEGIES

QUESTION

Are the basic strategies for online blackjack played differently than those worked out for land-based casinos, even though the "decks" in the online game are reshuffled each round? In other words, do I use the same strategies?

ANSWER

If the rules are the same and the simulations for number of decks are the same, then the strategies are the same. That online casinos shuffle after every hand, thus giving you a fresh pack of cards to start with, is exactly what basic strategy assumes anyway.

3. STRATEGY WHEN SHUFFLING MACHINES ARE USED

QUESTION

I have enthusiastically learned your basic strategies and I also ordered your card counting strategies—which worked out great for me, by the way! But there are new shuffling machines in the casino where I usually play and they shuffle the cards constantly. Every time a round is over, the used cards are put back into the shuffling machine. In my view, card counting isn't possible at this casino.

Here's my question: Am I correct that I cannot count cards when they use the shuffling machine?

ANSWER

Unfortunately, when the casino shuffles every time a round is completed, you cannot count cards, as you correctly surmised. Card counting is a strategy that takes advantage of the ten richness or poorness in a depleted pack of cards, using the change in composition of the remaining cards to get an edge. If a constant shuffling machine is used, the best you can do is play a perfect basic strategy. When you go on vacation to casinos that offer blackjack games without shuffling machines, as in most places, you will be able to effectively use card counting.

4. THE EFFECT OF THE GAME'S BETTING LIMIT

QUESTION

I live in an area where the maximum dollar amount you can bet per hand is $5. Any advice on how to handle strategy when the maximum amount is this small?

ANSWER

The amount of money at stake has no bearing on the proper strategy you should play. It's all relative. Whether the bet is $5 or $1,000, the same strategies apply.

5. PLAYING A SOFT 20

QUESTION

I understand all of your strategies so far except for the soft 20 against a dealer's 5 or 6. I know that the soft 20 is a very good hand, but wouldn't I be better off playing the A-9 as a 10 and doubling down just like I would if I had any hard 10?

ANSWER

The essential difference between the two hands is that with a soft 20 (A-9), you *already* have a point total of 20, a great hand. You don't want to ruin this near-sure win any more than you want to split a made 20 of two picture cards and turn it into two 10s as starting hands. Mathematically, you will make more money in the long run by taking the winning hand and collecting your win than you will by breaking up a 20 into two very strong hands, but ones that need draws to win.

The hard 10, on the other hand, must be drawn to anyway. With such a nice edge over the dealer, doubling on it is the correct, and very profitable, move.

6. COMING TO GRIPS WITH 12 VERSUS 2

QUESTION

I'm pretty comfortable with much of the basic strategy, but there's one play I just can't come to grips with. The scenario: I have a 12 versus the dealer's 2. I know I'm supposed to hit, but I hate busting first, especially when the dealer ends up busting afterwards. I primarily sit in the third-base spot and play multiple-deck games. I've got some big trips coming up and would like to get completely sold on the "why" before traveling.

ANSWER

The hand 12 versus 2 is not as close a decision as the 16 versus 10 would be. Only a 10 will bust you, and if the dealer is holding a 12, only a 10 would bust him too, at least on the first draw. The combination of busting less on both ends makes the 12 versus 2 a clear hitting decision. It doesn't matter whether you're on first base, third base or in the middle—you have about a 4% gain in doing this. Of course, you never want to bust first, but there is a very big difference between drawing to a 12 and drawing to a 14, for example. With a 14, you have the 8s and 9s that would bust the hand on the draw, cards that a 12 would love to see.

You have to think in terms of the percentages when playing blackjack, not how you feel or what happened on the previous hand or few hands. So, if you do hit on a 12 versus 2 and bust, you cannot alter your strategy just because "the play didn't work the last time I tried it." It may not work the next time or the time after that, but if you play with the percentages, they will work for you over the long run. You cannot look at the short-term results of blackjack or anything else in gambling—not if you want to win. You must always make the best plays to have the best chances of being a winner.

7. PROTECTING AGAINST THAT ONE BAD SESSION

QUESTION

I started playing blackjack on a semi-professional level and encountered the following problem. My first two weeks, I was just awesome playing two sessions a day, sometimes three. I started out winning seven sessions in a row, split the next six, won three in a row, lost four, then won six out of the next ten times. But on the third week, everything just fell apart. I lost more times than I won, which wouldn't have been so bad except for one really big losing session that wiped out *all* of my wins.

I was doing so good, then suddenly it all fell apart. What went wrong?

ANSWER

Several problems contributed to your downfall. For the most part, this big dive could have been avoided. First, you likely became tired after all that effort at the table, which could have negatively impacted your decision-making. Fatigue typically leads to strategy mistakes and giving the edge back to the house. Once you start losing, bad decisions seem to feed off of other bad decisions, causing poor percentage plays, mistakes and, ultimately, losses.

Even worse is your second mistake, and it's a critical one. Sessions that should have ended positively, or at least not too negatively, become protracted sessions with painful losses. It is normal to wear out at anything—blackjack included. The trick is to recognize weariness and to react intelligently by taking a break until you feel refreshed. It is hard to maintain confidence and concentration during a losing run. You went wrong here by stubbornly playing on when you weren't feeling strong. Never let yourself take a big beating in any one session.

Nightmarish losses are hard to recover from, financially as well as emotionally.

It sounds like you play a pretty good blackjack game. Now, just fix these leaks and your results will be much more pleasing.

8. PLAYING MULTIPLE HANDS

QUESTION

Do I have better odds playing multiple hands at blackjack as opposed to just one hand? I'm always tempted to play more than one hand, but I don't know if it's a good idea or not.

ANSWER

In terms of your chances of winning, it makes no difference whether you play one hand, two hands, or all hands on the table. The odds remain the same. The cards don't know whether you're playing that second hand or another player is, nor do they know whether you're sitting in the first seat or the third one. One seat has no better odds than another.

The number of hands you play is a money management issue. The more money you have on the table, the more money you have at risk. For example, if you had enough chips to withstand 16 losses and played all seven spots on a table, doubling down on one hand and splitting another, you'd be wiped out if the dealer drew a blackjack the first time and a 20 the second time (assuming you didn't draw that or better as well). Two hands, you'd be gone.

It comes back to playing in your comfort zone. It's okay to play two (or more) hands at a time—if playing two hands simultaneously doesn't stretch you thin, you don't mind a little extra flux, and the bets fit within your bankroll capabilities.

9. THE TRICKY EIGHTS PLAY: WHO'S RIGHT?

QUESTION

I've been playing for only one month and always stand on two eights when I get them against a 10. My friend, who's a little more experienced than me, says it's the wrong play, that I should be drawing a card to try to improve. But with so many cards busting the 16, that seems like a worse play. Who's right?

ANSWER

Actually, neither of you is right. The proper play is to split your 8s into two hands of 8 each. Here's the deal: A 16 is a lousy hand and you're going to lose about three out of four times by standing or drawing, with drawing being a slightly better play. And while two hands of 8 each also have losing expectations, together they are an improvement over your 16 versus 10 draw (or stand) play.

10. PLAYING WITH BAD AMATEURS

QUESTION

I hate playing with amateur players at my table. Last trip I had a big double down and this new player sits down and busts a 16 against a dealer's 6. The dealer turns over a 10 for his own 16, hits a 5, and everybody at the table loses. How can I avoid playing with bad players at my table? They always seem to ruin my hands.

ANSWER

In the long run, the last player has absolutely no effect on what card the dealer will draw. It will help you as often as it will go against you. It makes no difference at all what any player at the table does. The cards don't know if you have Joe Blow on third base, or blackjack legend Arnold Snyder. And what either one of them do won't hurt or help you over the long haul. You just remember the painful times when things didn't go well and not the times where they saved your big bets.

What matters most is that you stick religiously to the proper strategy, and never alter your play—and your best odds—no matter how things are going. But if playing with bad players bothers you, switch tables where you won't have to deal with worrying about what other players do.

BONUS QUESTION: THINKING ABOUT PLAYING BLACKJACK PROFESSIONALLY

QUESTION

I'm a fairly normal guy in the real world, but when it comes to gambling, particularly blackjack, I get pretty worked up with the thrills. I know I can beat the game. I've studied all sorts of blackjack books and advanced strategies and have the game down pat. I'm thinking, if I can get on rolls like I do sometimes, I can pile up a whole bunch of money quickly and play professionally. What do you think?

ANSWER

I caution you that blackjack is not a get-rich-quick scheme, nor is it an easy way to make a living, even if you have an edge over the casino. Ups and downs are part of any form of gambling, and if you can't emotionally handle the downswings—and very few players can—you'll end up a loser, no matter how good you are. Losing streaks are part of any form of gambling. Pros can weather these tough times and still be around for the winning streaks. It's all about emotional control and money management.

Very simple advice for you: Start with small stakes, and prove you can win before increasing the amount at stake. And if you've proven to be a consistent winner over a period of time, then you can think about taking things to the next level.

GLOSSARY

Barring a Player

The exclusion of a player from the blackjack tables when casino personnel feel a player is too skillful.

Basic Strategy

The optimal playing strategy for a particular set of rules and number of decks used, assuming the player has knowledge of only his own two cards and the dealer's upcard.

Blackjack or Natural

An original two card holding consisting of an ace and 10-value card. Also the name of the game.

Break

see B*ust*.

Burn Card

A card from the top of the deck that is removed from play. The top card is traditionally *burned* after a fresh shuffle and before the cards are dealt.

Bust or Break

To exceed the total of 21, an automatic loser.

Card Counting

A method of keeping track of the cards already played so that knowledge of the remaining cards can be used to adjust strategies. A player that counts cards is called a *card counter*.

Composition of the Deck

A term used to describe the particular makeup of the cards remaining in the deck.

Composition Change

As cards are removed from the deck, the normal proportion of certain cards to other groups of cards change. This is called a composition change.

Dealer

The casino employee who deals the cards, makes the proper payoffs to winning hands and collects lost bets.

Doubling, Doubling Down

A player option to double the original bet after seeing his original two cards. If the player chooses this option, one additional card will be dealt.

Doubling After Splitting

Option only infrequently offered in casinos whereby players are allowed to double down after splitting a pair (according to normal doubling rules).

Draw

see *Hit*.

Early Surrender

An option to forfeit a hand and lose half the bet before the dealer checks for a blackjack. As opposed to *Late Surrender*.

Exposed Card

see *Upcard*.

Eye in the Sky

Refers to the mirrors above the gaming tables where the games are constantly supervised to protect both the player and the house from being cheated.

Face Card

Also known as *Paint*. A jack, queen or king.

First Base
Seat closest to the dealer's left. The first baseman acts upon his hand first. As opposed to *Third Base*.

Flat Bet
To bet the same amount every hand.

Gravitate
The tendency of a hand to improve to a total that is 10 points higher after the drawing of cards. For example, a two-card 9 tends to gravitate towards a 19.

Hard Total
A hand without an ace or if containing an ace, where the ace counts as only 1 point. For example, 97, K6 and 5AQ are all hard 16s. As opposed to *Soft Total*.

Head On or Head-to-Head
Playing alone against the dealer.

High Roller
A player that wagers big money.

Hit
The act of drawing (requesting) a card from the dealer.

Hole Card
The dealer's unexposed downcard.

House
A term to denote the casino.

Insurance
A side bet that can be made when the dealer shows an ace. The player wagers up to half his original bet and gets paid 2 to 1 on that bet if the dealer shows a blackjack. If the dealer does not have a blackjack, the insurance bet is lost. Play continues as usual.

Late Surrender
A player option to forfeit his original hand and lose half the bet after it has been determined that the dealer does not have

a blackjack. Option offered in some casinos. As opposed to *Early Surrender*.

Marker

An IOU signed by a player with established credit at a casino.

Multiple-Deck Game

Blackjack played with two or more decks of cards, usually referring to a 4, 6 or 8 deck game. As opposed to *Single Deck*.

Natural

see *Blackjack*.

Nickels

$5 chips, usually red in color.

Northern Nevada

Usually referring to Lake Tahoe and Reno but can include other casino locations in Northern Nevada.

Pat Card

A dealer upcard of 7 through ace, one that tends to give the dealer pat hands.

Pat Hand

A hand totalling 17-21.

Pit Boss

Casino employee who supervises play at the gaming tables.

Push

A tie between the dealer and the player. Neither side wins.

Quarters

$25 chips, usually green in color.

Resplit

To split identically-ranked cards after two cards were already split. For example, if you split 7-7, and receive a 7 as the first card on one of the split 7s, you may resplit the hand again.

Shoe
An oblong box used to hold multiple decks of cards. All 4 and 6 deck games are dealt out of a shoe.

Shuffle, Shuffling Up
The mixing of cards by a dealer prior to a fresh round of play.

Silver
$1 tokens or dollar chips.

Single-Deck Game
Blackjack played from a single pack of cards. As opposed to *Multiple Deck*.

Soft Hand, Soft Total
Hand in which the ace counts as 11 points. As opposed to *Hard Total*.

Splitting Pairs
A player option to split two cards of identical value so that two separate hands are formed. A bet equal to the original wager is placed next to the second hand.

Stand, Stand Pat
A player's decision not to draw a card.

Stiff Card
A dealer upcard of 2 through 6, one that leaves the dealer with a high busting potential.

Stiff Hand
A hand totalling hard 12, 13, 14, 15 or 16; can be busted if hit.

Surrender
See *Late Surrender*; *Early Surrender*. Usually refers to *Late Surrender*.

Ten Factor
Refers to the concentration of tens in the deck.

Ten Poor

Refers to a low proportion of 10-value cards remaining in play.

Ten Rich

Refers to a high proportion of 10-value cards remaining in play and their effect on strategy.

10-Value Card

10, jack, queen or king.

Third Base

Also called *Anchorman*. Position closest to the dealer's right. The third baseman makes the last play before the dealer's turn. As opposed to *First Base*.

Toke or Tip

A gratuity either given or bet for the dealer.

Unit

Bet size used as a standard of measurement.

Upcard

The dealer's face up (exposed) card.

BACCARAT MASTER CARD COUNTER
New Winning Strategy!

For the **first time**, GRI releases the **latest winning techniques** for making money at baccarat. This **exciting copyrighted** strategy, played by **big money players** in Monte Carlo and other exclusive locations, is **not available anywhere else**. Based on the same principles that have made insiders and pros **hundreds of thousands of dollars** at blackjack—card counting!

MATHEMATICALLY TESTED
Filled with charts for **easy reference and understanding**. Contains the most thorough mathematical **analysis** of baccarat in print (though explained in terms anyone can understand). You'll see exactly how this strategy works.

SIMPLE TO USE, EASY TO MASTER
You'll learn how to count cards without the mental effort needed for blackjack! No need to memorize numbers—keep the count on the scorepad. Easy-to-use, play the strategy while enjoying the game!

LEARN WHEN TO BET BANKER, PLAYER
No more hunch bets—use the *Baccarat Master Card Counter* to determine **when to bet Player or Banker**. You learn the basic counts (running and true), deck favorability, symmetrical vs. non-symmetrical play, when to increase bets and much **more** in this **winning strategy**.

PLAY SCIENTIFICALLY TO WIN
Drawing and standing advantage, average edge, average gain, total gain, win-loss and % of occurrence are shown for every relevant hand. You won't need to know these numbers or percentages, but we've included them here so you see exactly how the strategy works. You'll be the best player at the table—after just one reading! Baccarat can be beaten. This strategy shows you how!

This copyrighted strategy can only be purchased from Cardoza Publishing

To order send just $50 by check or money order to:
Cardoza Publishing, P.O. Box 98115, Las Vegas, NV 89193

POWERFUL WINNING POKER SIMULATIONS

A MUST FOR SERIOUS PLAYERS WITH A COMPUTER!
IBM compatible CD ROM Win 95, 98, 2000, NT, ME, XP

These incredible full color poker simulations are the best method to improve your game. Computer opponents play like real players. All games let you set the limits and rake and have fully programmable players, stat tracking, and Hand Analyzer for starting hands. Mike Caro, the world's foremost poker theoretician says, "Amazing... a steal for under $500... get it, it's great." Includes free phone support. "Smart Advisor" gives expert advice for every play!

1. TURBO TEXAS HOLD'EM FOR WINDOWS - $59.95. Choose which players, and how many (2-10) you want to play, create loose/tight games, and control check-raising, bluffing, position, sensitivity to pot odds, and more! Also, instant replay, pop-up odds, Professional Advisor keeps track of play statistics. Free bonus: Hold'em Hand Analyzer analyzes all 169 pocket hands in detail and their win rates under any conditions you set. Caro says this "hold'em software is the most powerful ever created." Great product!

2. TURBO SEVEN-CARD STUD FOR WINDOWS - $59.95. Create any conditions of play; choose number of players (2-8), bet amounts, fixed or spread limit, bring-in method, tight/loose conditions, position, reaction to board, number of dead cards, and stack deck to create special conditions. Features instant replay. Terrific stat reporting includes analysis of starting cards, 3-D bar charts, and graphs. Play interactively and run high speed simulation to test strategies. Hand Analyzer analyzes starting hands in detail. Wow!

3. TURBO OMAHA HIGH-LOW SPLIT FOR WINDOWS - $59.95. Specify any playing conditions; betting limits, number of raises, blind structures, button position, aggressiveness/ passiveness of opponents, number of players (2-10), types of hands dealt, blinds, position, board reaction, and specify flop, turn, and river cards! Choose opponents and use provided point count or create your own. Statistical reporting, instant replay, pop-up odds high speed simulation to test strategies, amazing Hand Analyzer, and much more!

4. TURBO OMAHA HIGH FOR WINDOWS - $59.95. Same features as above, but tailored for Omaha High only. Caro says program is "an electrifying research tool...it can clearly be worth thousands of dollars to any serious player." A must for Omaha High players.

5. TURBO 7 STUD 8 OR BETTER - $59.95. Brand new with all the features you expect from the Wilson Turbo products: the latest artificial intelligence, instant advice and exact odds, play versus 2-7 opponents, enhanced data charts that can be exported or printed, the ability to fold out of turn and immediately go to the next hand, ability to peek at opponents hand, optional warning mode that warns you if a play disagrees with the advisor, and automatic mode that runs up to 50 tests unattended. Tough computer players vary their styles for a great game.

---

6. TOURNAMENT TEXAS HOLD'EM - $39.95
Set-up for tournament practice and play, this realistic simulation pits you against celebrity look-alikes. Tons of options let you control tournament size with 10 to 300 entrants, select limits, ante, rake, blind structures, freezeouts, number of rebuys and competition level of opponents. Pop-up status report shows how you're doing vs. the competition. Save tournaments in progress to play again later. Additional feature allows quick folds on finished hands.